Krishnamurti for Beginners

An Anthology

KATHRYN CRAGGS.

Krishnamurti for Beginners

An Anthology

Krishnamurti Foundation India

Published by

Krishnamurti Foundation India
'Vasanta Vihar' 64 Greenways Road
Chennai - 600 028
Tel : 4937803 / 4937596
E-mail : kfihq@md2.vsnl.net.in

ISBN 81-87326-01-8
Philosophy / Religion

First Edition 1995
Reprinted 1995, 1998

Compiled by K. Krishnamurthy
Design and Layout by Vikram Parchure

Printed by
Sudarsan Graphics,
14, Neelakanda Mehta Street
T. Nagar, Chennai - 600 017

Preface

Krishnamurti for Beginners is an introduction to the teachings of J. Krishnamurti, meant primarily for readers unacquainted with his work. The problems of daily living that confront every human being and Krishnamurti's original approach to them form the basis of the selections.

The Anthology encompasses a variety of genres — public talks, answers to questions, writings, interviews, diaries, dictations, letters, dialogues and discussions — in which Krishnamurti presented his central vision of life. They range over the most significant period of his teachings, from 1948 to 1983.

Krishnamurti held that truth is beyond the constructions of the human mind, beyond 'the known, formulated or imagined', and that in the search for truth 'the first step is the last step'. In the sense that new beginnings held a special meaning for Krishnamurti, all are beginners on the journey of life. And in this sense, the present volume is meant for all.

A biographical essay reviews Krishnamurti's early life and sketches the historical background which informed his later teachings. The essay attempts to uncover, within Krishnamurti's formative years, the creative springs of his life and philosophy.

Contents

Krishnamurti : The Formative Years

When Victoria was Empress of India, a boy was born in one of Her Majesty's more remote provinces. The year was 1895, the place was Madanapalle — a town in the Cuddappah District of Madras Presidency. The boy's father, a Telugu Brahmin named Jiddu Narayaniah, held a modest position in the District Revenue Department. The child was called Krishnamurti (Krishna incarnate).

Fifty years earlier, Thomas Babbington Macaulay had led a public debate on the future of education in India. Macaulay's firm support for English as the medium of instruction was based on ideals of progress. Comparing nineteenth century India with mediaeval Europe, Macaulay asked rhetorically whether public funds should be used to teach a dying tradition in a dead language. For Macaulay, all questions of educational policy for India resolved into one great choice: English or Sanskrit; Newton or Ptolemy; Adam Smith or the Vedas; Milton or *Mahabharata*; modern or mediaeval medicine; an earth in motion or the sun orbiting a stationary earth.

C.E. Trevelyan, architect of the Indian civil service and Macaulay's brother-in-law, drew out the details of an imperial *quid pro quo* :

> The British had nothing to give to the Indians except their superior knowledge: Everything else — revenues, honours, private emoluments — was taken from them but in the end the greater proportion of the advantages which the British gained would be amply repaid.

India would surrender freedom and material resources in exchange for the future benefits of European culture and knowledge.

These Victorians, men of liberal temperament, were devoted to ideals of reason, progress, liberty and human perfectibility. Their country had been in the vanguard of advancing scientific thought and had played a leading role in the Industrial Revolution. Against this background they could find little or nothing worth salvaging from Indian traditions. Macaulay held the history of Britain since the beginning of the seventeenth century to be a history of 'physical, moral and intellectual improvement', without finding any comparable progress in India. Trevelyan conceded that India's past must 'of course' be studied, but only 'for antiquarian reasons'. These guardians of the Empire were moved by a sense of destiny that Victoria's Poet Laureate Alfred Lord Tennyson captured in his rousing verse:

> Not in vain the distance beacons,
> Forward, forward let us range,
> Let the great world spin for ever
> Down the ringing grooves of change

Not everyone agreed with those who won the day for Western education and the English language in India. Some, like the eminent Orientalist H.H. Wilson, founder of Sanskrit College in Calcutta, believed that material for a new India could be found in India's own past. Wilson maintained that European science and learning could help India reconstruct its past and thereby recover its own sources of 'intellectual and moral improvement'. Advocates and opponents alike agreed on the merits of Western scientific method and rationality for advancement of society. That shared assumption was implicit both in Macaulay's way of contrasting contemporary science with mediaeval doctrine, and in Wilson's decision to introduce mechanics, hydraulics and optics into the Sanskrit College curriculum.

This unequal contest between European and Indian culture occurred within a colonial context, with all the ambiguities and tensions inherent in relations between a dominant power and its subjugated peoples. But Macaulay's choice of modernity over tradition persuaded Indian intellectuals like Raja Ram Mohun Roy that European culture was the order of the day for India.

❖

Krishnamurti's parents were far removed from this debate on the larger canvas of India. As Brahmins, they represented a long tradition of literary and priestly learning, but his grandfather and great-grandfather, responding to changing times, had ventured outside the traditional patterns of Indian life, finding employment on the fringes of the wider and still alien English-speaking world. Despite this they retained their orthodox roots, and remained faithful to the ritual cycles that unite a Brahmin's daily life with family, community and cosmos.

The home life of a typical Brahmin household in the nineteenth century was an enclosed world, self-sufficient and whole in its cyclical rhythms. Sons in particular were swaddled in protection: ritual ceremonies, presided over by gods and goddesses, offered them shelter from unknown terrors. Sons were seldom allowed to be frustrated. We are told that an astrologer was called in to draw up Krishnamurti's horoscope the day after he was born, and a great future was forecast for him. In due course, in keeping with ancient traditions, Krishnamurti was initiated into the life of learning by ceremonially tracing the symbol *Aum* on a silver platter covered with rice for the occasion.

As an officer in the Revenue Department, Krishnamurti's father was away from home a great deal. Krishnamurti's mother, Sanjivamma, a religious woman of gentle and generous temperament, was devoted to her family and to the worship of Lord Krishna. With her eldest daughter's assistance she created a warm and devout household for her large family of sons and daughters — other children, including Nityananda, having been born after Krishnamurti.

Ritual is a birthright, but the religious temper is a gift unequally distributed among the members of a family. Nitya was destined for studies even before he was old enough to be enrolled in school, while Krishnamurti, kept from school by malaria, was drawn into a community of shared religious feeling created by his devout mother. She read him stories from the *Mahabharata* and the *Ramayana*. Together they climbed a small hilltop shrine and partook of visions of Lord Krishna. Much later in life Krishnamurti set aside such visions as products of conditioning — had he been born a Christian he might have had visions of Jesus. Nonetheless in Sanjivamma's generosity of spirit there was a lesson that Krishnamurti didn't entirely learn but never completely forgot. Narayaniah described Krishnamurti's uncertain induction into the daily ritual of charity practised by the orthodox:

> In the morning when beggars come to the house, it is our custom to send out to them a cup or bowl of unboiled rice, and we distribute it to the hands outheld in turn, until the cup is empty. My wife would send Krishna out to give the alms, and the little fellow would come back for more, saying he had poured it all into one man's bag. Then his mother would go with him and teach him how to give to each.

A photograph of Krishnamurti at the age of two shows a clear-eyed, outgoing child engaging the camera with affectionate gaze. The child grew into a tenderhearted and generous boy who was frequently ill with malaria and had difficulties with school lessons. He could not follow the lessons or keep up with the class, and was often mistreated by his teachers.

The happiest memories of Krishnamurti's early life centred around his mother. But that period of secure home life ended with the loss of both his mother and his beloved sister when he was barely ten years old. 'My mother's death in 1905 deprived my brothers and myself of the one who loved and cared for us most, and my father was too much occupied to pay much attention to us,' Krishnamurti wrote eight years after the event, adding 'there was really nobody to look after us.'

❖

Religion is one of the most mysterious of human impulses. Etymologically the word derives from a root that means 'to bind'. At one level religion binds men and women to a larger community. At another level it ties them to a divine principle, as sacred rituals mark the great events of life, birth, entry into adulthood, marriage and death. Emotions felt on these occasions may be shared by the community, externalized, and at turning points in life, a unity of shared feeling may overcome one's sense of isolation. Religious songs, myths and rituals may express collective memories of anxieties, triumphs, fears and hopes. Unknown priests, poets and artists have contributed to this tradition. Faith and codified beliefs characterize a stage in religions as they seek to extend their boundaries and bring new converts into the fold.

Twenty years before Krishnamurti's birth, a movement called Theosophy had been started in America in a spirit of reaction against materialism and contemporary scientific humanism. Its founder, a Russian clairvoyant named Helena Petrovna Blavatsky, vigorously denied the evolution of human beings from apes, and accused Christianity of distorting the message of Christ. She promised a 'synthesis of science, religion and philosophy' based on the application of clairvoyant powers in exploring 'the hidden mysteries of nature and the hidden powers of man'.

Although Blavatsky intensely disliked Darwin's version of evolution, the idea of evolutionary progress so central to the later nineteenth century resonated through her thought, which she expressed in her own scientific-sounding vocabulary. She considered human life to be one stage in a progression 'upwards' from a 'terrestrial' to a 'celestial' plane, and she was confident that scientific truth, the past and the future were all open tc clairvoyant inspection. In the words of a follower:

> We find that as there are definite stages in the earlier evolution – vegetable above the mineral, the animal over the vegetable and the human above the animal – so in the same way the human kingdom has a definite end, a boundary at which it passes into a kingdom distinctly higher than itself, that beyond men there are Supermen.

Blavatsky borrowed very freely from Buddhist, Hindu and many other sources. Karma, rebirth, and release from bondage all figure in her writings, along with spiritual guides to lead the way to freedom. A true spiritual guide, according to her doctrine, was to be:

> A man of profound knowledge, exoteric and esoteric, especially the latter, and one who has brought this carnal knowledge under the subjection of the will; who has developed in himself both the power *(siddhi)* to control the forces of Nature, and the capacity to probe her secrets by the help of the formerly latent but now active powers of his being.

— that is, a person who is equipped to challenge the authority of both dogmatic religion and materialistic science in their own domains, by exercise of will and with the help of occult powers.

In 1882 Blavatsky moved the headquarters of the Theosophical Society to India because, in Theosophical doctrine, the Himalayas had been the home of powerful

Masters. A spacious estate was chosen on the outskirts of the city of Madras. Its grounds were lush with coconut fronds and venerable banyan trees; they were bordered by the Adyar river on one side and the Bay of Bengal on another. In the course of time many shrines, temples, churches and mosques, cast in the eclectic Theosophical mould, were constructed within the Adyar estate.

The Society's presence on Indian soil was like a window with many prospects. The Indian upper classes, subjects of a partly Anglicized world, who had seen their religion and their arts scorned, and who had learned to measure their own culture by foreign yardsticks, found in the Society's doctrines a compelling vision of their own spiritual past, freed from its archaic and provincial elements, made cosmopolitan, contemporary, and therefore whole. They were drawn in large numbers to the Society's fold. Christian missionaries were dismayed to see Europeans attracted to beliefs of the very colonials they were engaged in converting. The government, suspicious of anything that might encourage nationalistic sentiment, shared the missionaries' misgivings. Orthodox Hindus also disapproved of the new movement, which they saw as debasing their old tradition.

Building a new religious movement involves a large-scale assembly of myths, rituals and a sense of community which are not easy to mobilize at short notice. Nonetheless, towards the closing years of the nineteenth century, when resurgent Europe had brought many diverse peoples under its colonial umbrella, a niche had opened up for a movement capable of establishing links between separate cultures — Eastern and Western — and between science and religion. The Theosophical programme of drawing these diverse spheres into a unified and peaceful brotherhood attracted a large membership from all over the world.

Annie Besant was one of those who were drawn to Theosophy in pursuit of these ideals. Before joining the movement, Mrs Besant had worked for virtually every radical social movement in England: she had fought on behalf of women's rights, for freethinkers and for trade unions, and was for some time an active member of the London School Board. When in 1879 she came under the spell of Helena Blavatsky, her attention turned to India and eventually she moved to Benares, the great centre of Hindu orthodoxy and learning – an intrepid move for a European woman. In Benares she began devoting her considerable energies to re-creating a new culture out of treasures from India's past. With the help of Sanskrit scholars, she brought out a translation of the *Bhagavad Gita,* and established schools and colleges in several parts of the country.

Mrs Besant was president of the Theosophical Society ("TS") when Krishnamurti's father Narayaniah, recently retired from Government service, offered to work for her as a clerk, in exchange for free food and accommodation. In 1909 Narayaniah brought his three children, a nephew and an elderly aunt to live in a tiny cottage outside the TS compound wall. He enrolled Krishnamurti and his younger brother Nitya in a school in Mylapore some distance away.

One day at Adyar, the two boys caught the attention of C.W. Leadbeater ("CWL"), an associate of Mrs Besant's in the Theosophical Society. Leadbeater sensed something unusual in the young Krishnamurti, which he later described as 'an aura with no trace of selfishness'. He wrote to Mrs Besant, who was in Europe at the time, telling her about Narayaniah and his family of well-behaved boys, and reporting that on investigation he had found Krishnamurti 'to have a past of very great importance, indicating far greater advancement than his father, or indeed than any of the people at present at Headquarters — a better set of lives even than Hubert.' This was a striking comparison, because the Theosophists were actively on the lookout for a Messiah, and Hubert [van Hook] was an American boy who at that time was already being groomed as a leading candidate for that position.

The coming of a Messiah had been predicted within several religious traditions. In one of the most famous passages of the *Bhagavad Gita,* Lord Krishna used these words to announce his own reappearance in each world epoch:

> When right conduct is destroyed and evil is on the ascendant, then I incarnate, in order to save the good, destroy evil and restore righteousness.

Judaism, Buddhism, Christianity and some sects within Islam have taught that one day a Messiah would appear to save the world from darkness. Under Mrs Besant's direction, Theosophy developed its own Messianic doctrine, and before long the young Krishnamurti was selected as a potential 'vehicle' for its realization.

Theosophical doctrine, made up eclectically from several religious traditions, settled in due course on the belief that if Krishnamurti was properly prepared, Lord Maitreya or the future Buddha would manifest in his body, and the Society undertook to prepare the world for this event.

Leadbeater's interest in Eastern mysticism coexisted with a domineering nature and strong colonial overtones. A love of high adventure and a strong imaginative flair coloured his memory so that the events in his own life seemed to grow ever more fabulous with the retelling. He was considered an adept in esoteric practices, including the reading of 'auras' and the telling of 'past lives'.

Soon after their first meeting, CWL asked Narayaniah to bring Krishnamurti to his bungalow. Seating the young boy beside him on a sofa, he dramatically placed a hand on his head and began recounting a set of intricately wrought tales of adventure and self-sacrifice, in which the central figure was Alcyone — a code name for Krishnamurti. This involved narrative was later transcribed and published as *The Lives of Alcyone*. Mrs Besant and other Theosophists appeared in these tales, in forms modified to suit various periods of history, on earth and on several other planets. Leadbeater arranged a reading of *The Lives* on an open terrace for an excited and marvelling audience.

Having invested Krishnamurti with a full set of past lives, CWL made every possible effort to draw the boy away from the life into which he was born, from his family and their dilapidated cottage outside the Theosophical Society compound. He began by persuading Narayaniah to remove his sons from the Mylapore school 'where they are being beaten by a teacher who ought to be selling bootlaces', and to place them in the charge of a small group of European teachers under his personal supervision. The boys were dressed in new clothes and given food of a kind that their father on his meagre pension could not afford. Their Brahmin knots were cut and the hair was grown out to shoulder length, brushed back and parted in the middle. They were taught to ride bicycles and play games. Each morning Leadbeater would ask them: 'Well, what do you remember from our activities during the night?' Shyly, in faulty English, they would give their report, and CWL would add some interesting details 'from the astral plane'.

Mrs Besant was introduced to Krishnamurti in November 1909. Less than a month afterwards she initiated him and Nityananda into the Esoteric Section, an inner group within the TS meant for the elect, who were to swear an oath of obedience to her and commit themselves unconditionally to the Coming of the World Teacher. Those who did not accept the idea — and there were many who did not — were consigned to a probationary class. Simultaneously Mrs Besant imposed the idea of a Spiritual Path with five graded stages leading from Initiate to Adept, as the central scale on which members were to be ranked. The authority to decide who occupied each spiritual level on the Path would reside with her and CWL.

At Leadbeater's bidding Mrs Besant persuaded Narayaniah to allow the boys to stay in a room close to hers, where she would read aloud to them and instruct them in spoken English. Shortly thereafter CWL arranged for a 'great audience with the Occult Powers', during which Kuthumi, one of the Masters of Theosophy, presented Krishnamurti to Lord Maitreya as 'a candidate who seeks admission to the Great Brotherhood'. With Kuthumi as his Master and with Leadbeater and Mrs Besant as guides on the 'upward way', Krishnamurti became a novitiate on the spiritual path. Krishnamurti described his introduction to these mysteries in a letter to Mrs Besant:

> Then the Lord spoke to me for the first time:- 'Do you on your own part love these two Brethren, so that you will gladly submit yourself to their guidance?' And, of course I answered:- 'Indeed I do love them with all my heart.' He asked:- 'You desire then to join the Brotherhood which exists from eternity unto eternity?' And I said:- 'I wish to join when I am fit to do so.' He asked:- 'Do you know the object of this Brotherhood?' I replied:- 'To do the work of the Logos by helping the world.' Then he replied:- 'Will you pledge yourself to devote all your life and all your strength henceforth to this work, forgetting yourself absolutely for the good of the world, making your life all love, even as He is all love?' And I answered:- 'I will, with the Master's help.' He continued:- 'Do you promise to keep secret those things which you are told to keep secret?' And I said:- 'I do promise.'

In this ceremony Krishnamurti, the champion of freedom and enquiry, was being pledged to their virtual opposites—submission and secrecy. The following year, he was made head of a study group which soon grew into an international organization, The Order of the Star in the East, the centre-piece of a rich context Mrs Besant and CWL were building up around him. George Arundale described their new Messianic cult in glowing terms:

> You know the level reached by our Chief — for members of our Group she and Mr Leadbeater represent to us the ideals of life in the world, and the more we trust and follow them the quicker progress shall we make and the better service render ... We are face to face with the world's most stirring period, a period which occurs but once every few thousand years; we are living in the midst — in the very midst so far as the Group is concerned — of all the preparations which are to precede the central point of the period; we meet in the flesh members of the real Fraternity whom two thousand years ago we should have called Apostles; we have John the Baptist and other disciples of the beloved Rishis.

All this extravagance had no visible effect on Krishnamurti himself. According to Wodehouse:

> We were older people, educationalists, and with some experience of youth. Had there been any trace in him of conceit or affectation, or any posing as the 'holy child', or priggish self consciousness, we would undoubtedly have given an adverse verdict.

Krishnamurti was by and large a pliant student, eager to please, but there was an aloofness about him and a certain vagueness — his vacant look — that infuriated Leadbeater. Once when Krishnamurti was staring into space with his mouth wide open, CWL lost control and struck him. It was a turning point for the young boy, and his relationship with Leadbeater was never the same. He never allowed himself to keep his mouth open, and, more importantly, a reflective and critical consciousness took hold within him. Looking back in old age at his fourteen-year-old self, Krishnamurti described a boy with an empty persona, rapt in the world: 'It was all there: the beach, the shells, the catamarans; he was *that*.' He thought CWL, lacking the sensitivity of a truly religious person, had missed something important about the young boy; perhaps a key to the boy's uniqueness lay in just this quality of vagueness — a space within his consciousness, an emptiness that was later to be known as the silent mind.

Narayaniah opposed CWL's efforts to steep the two boys in esoteric practices and wrench them away from their family and cultural roots. It was no secret that some years earlier, CWL had been accused of misconduct, and in the ensuing furore had been obliged to resign from the Theosophical Society for some time. Now, with the help of orthodox Hindus from Madras, Narayaniah filed a suit reviving those earlier charges and reclaiming custody of his two sons on the ground that Mrs Besant had violated their agreement by allowing the boys to fall under CWL's tutelage.

Mrs Besant eloquently argued her own defence but lost the custody case, even though the charges against Leadbeater were not sustained. She filed an appeal with the Privy Council, and then had the boys removed to England before a new verdict could be handed down. Thus ended the first phase of Krishnamurti's life — a phase when a vague and unfocussed child with no well-defined sense of self was removed from his traditional milieu and trained to be the World Teacher.

❖

At this point it may be useful to contrast Mrs Besant's attitudes to Krishnamurti and the cult of the World Teacher with those of Leadbeater. Even though Mrs Besant trusted CWL and even though there was remarkably little public division between them, they each saw Krishnamurti's role in a different light.

Leadbeater was a self-made man in a special nineteenth century sense. Like John James Audubon and Sir Henry Stanley, men of great energy but modest social standing, he had reconstructed his own life with much imagination and considerable flair. In late nineteenth century Europe, the invention of lives had become a highly developed form of art. CWL was eminently skilled in this genre, and Krishnamurti as Messiah was his master-work.

Mrs Besant was a public figure fully engaged on the large political canvas of India's freedom movement, who counted Bernard Shaw, H. G. Wells and Mahatma Gandhi among her friends. She did not seek personal fulfilment through Theosophy. If Krishnamurti was to be the World Teacher, she would do her utmost to protect him, to educate him, to provide him with intellectual skills and a grace of manner that would command respect. Her overwhelming concern was to surround him with worthy disciples, who would respect and look after him. Though Krishnamurti disagreed with. her, he never questioned Mrs Besant's authenticity or the genuineness of her feelings towards him.

Leadbeater derived authority for much of his practice from specific and often implausibly detailed 'instructions from the Masters'. On Master Kuthumi's authority he was 'told':

> to civilize them; to teach them to use spoons and forks, nail brushes and toothbrushes, to sit at ease upon chairs instead of crouching on the ground, to sleep rationally on a bed, not in a corner like a dog.

These instructions identified civilized behaviour with European ways, in particular with the style and manners of upper class English society. Even though recent scholarship casts doubt on Leadbeater's own claims to social standing, there would have been many Indians, Americans and members of the Russian aristocracy of this period who shared his high evaluation of the English upper crust. And CWL had been urging Mrs Besant to send the boys to England even before the custody battle provided its own reasons for that move.

With this colonial model in mind, a suitable course of study was drawn up for the two brothers. They were to be tutored for entrance to the great universities of England. Their pierced earlobes were to be sown. They learned to wear shoes that would have hurt their feet, to do cross-country runs, and to eat breakfasts of porridge and eggs they would find hard to digest. They would have riding lessons, sail boats in Kensington Gardens and play croquet on manicured lawns during long summer evenings in the late setting sun. They were taken to the theatre, to cricket matches, and to the London Zoo. They were fitted for elegant clothes by Savile Row tailors. An Earl's wife and a Viceroy's daughter helped to care for the two boys and to link them with aristocratic society.

The England to which Krishnamurti was introduced was breaking out of the smugness of Victorian life. Widening prosperity had helped foster a liberal, progressive and intellectually scintillating culture. Even though barbaric forces of destruction were soon to be set loose in the First World War, there was a feeling in the air 'that human beings might really be on the brink of becoming civilized'. These hopes for a 'society which was free, rational, civilized, pursuing truth and beauty', were inspired in part by socialist ideals of equality and justice, and were fostered by the political writings of Bernard Shaw, H.G. Wells, Sidney and Beatrice Webb, members of the Fabian Society and friends of Mrs Besant. The philosophers Bertrand Russell and G.E. Moore, the writers Virginia and Leonard Woolf, T.S. Eliot and E.M. Forster, were all challenging what they felt were worn-out Victorian conventions. Elsewhere in Europe, passions that formerly had gone into preparing for an afterlife now began to be directed against the social framework.

Though Krishnamurti spent the next nine years in Europe, he was not drawn into these new intellectual movements, nor was he attracted by current movements in art and literature. Unlike the romantic student revolutionaries of that time, Krishnamurti remained a spectator, witnessing the horrors of the First World War, the dangerous promise of the Russian revolution, and the euphoria of peace under The League of Nations, in human rather than in ideological terms.

Krishnamurti's world at first seemed to revolve around his tutors, C. Jinarajadasa and George Arundale, older Theosophists and close associates of Mrs Besant and CWL, who had both been persuaded to interrupt their own academic work in order to steer Krishnamurti through entrance examinations for Oxford University. These two were later replaced by a succession of other tutors who struggled in vain to interest Krishnamurti in mathematics, or the history of ideas, or political theory — all hopeless efforts. Their young student had absolutely no head for examinations. The creative ferment in Europe, issues engaging the best minds of the time, made no impact on him. Nothing seemed to take root in his mind. But he had a good ear for languages and he loved poetry. With Oxford now beyond reach, he was sent to Paris to learn French and study music.

Krishnamurti was a handsomely dressed, debonair young man, shy but full of boyish merriment when at ease. Underneath this winning exterior was a young observer of the human condition who questioned many things, including the role that had been thrust on him and the pomp and ceremony that went with it. His portrait reveals an exceedingly romantic looking young man gazing into the distance — detached, slightly lost, as if he did not quite belong; with neither the confidence nor the self-absorption of a person who knew his place in the world.

❖

Resistance to Leadbeater and to his plans had become manifest in Krishnamurti by the age of eighteen, even as his father's custody suit was in progress. In a letter to CWL he wrote:

> I think it is time now that I should take my affairs into my own hands. I feel I would carry out the Master's instructions better if they were not forced upon me and made unpleasant as they have been for some years... I have not been given any opportunity to feel my responsibilities and I have been dragged about like a baby.

By 1920 Krishnamurti had doubts about the application of Theosophy to human problems. Mentioning a young acquaintance who had lost someone she loved, he wrote:

> When a most critical moment comes Theosophy and all its innumerable books don't help. She wants to see the Masters physically or mentally & she does not believe what A. B. and C.W.L. have said, in fact she feels what we [Nitya and I] have felt for the last two or three years... I tried to persuade her from not waking occult powers & and all that kind of thing but she is longing for it.

After a decade of training to be the World Teacher, Krishnamurti saw that the esoteric doctrines and occult powers of Theosophy had no healing touch to offer this young woman in her 'most critical moment'— paralysed by earlier misfortune and now bereaved by recent loss. Without being able to offer an effective alternative at that time, Krishnamurti felt desolate. But a conviction was growing — that religion should directly address the human condition of sorrow. This conviction was not based on ideology or exposure to philosophy, but on an intuitive awareness which he carried within him like a touchstone.

After nine years in Europe Krishnamurti had lost contact with his native traditions, without finding any satisfactory replacement for them in the West. And the occult world held no charm for him. In the winter of 1921, then twenty-six years old, he returned to India for a brief stopover en route to Australia. Accompanying him on the long journey was Nitya, in failing health from progressive tuberculosis.

In Madras to address the annual Theosophical Convention, Krishnamurti made what must have been a last visit to his father's home. The meeting was not a success. There are conflicting reports about what actually happened, but having prostrated himself at his father's feet in the traditional manner, Krishnamurti came away convinced that Narayaniah felt polluted by the touch of his 'foreign' sons. Having become a man without history and without direction, in early 1922 Krishnamurti sought retreat in Ojai, California, in a remote valley with a dry climate and a quiet atmosphere, in which Nitya might recuperate, and Krishnamurti would study and meditate.

Thus began a momentous year in his life. The person who sat under the shade of a pepper tree in Ojai, 'happy beyond all human happiness' was quite different from the bored young man who had been dragged through Europe failing one examination after another. During those earlier years he may have felt occasional intimations of his destiny; but from now onward he was sure of his direction in life and pursued it without hesitation.

One year earlier he had written to a friend: 'I don't know the philosophy of my life but I *will* have one... I must find myself, then *only* can I help others.' But long after the great experience which was soon to engulf him, long after his philosophy was fully developed, he retained the sense that life was a mystery and our place in it was a discovery for each of us to make anew.

Our knowledge of what transpired in Ojai between August 1922 and March 1923 is based largely on Nitya's notes and on letters the two brothers wrote to Mrs Besant and CWL. Nitya felt he was witnessing sacred rites in which unseen powers were preparing his brother's body to receive Lord Maitreya — as though what Leadbeater had predicted in 1909 was finally coming true.

It is not very easy for modern readers to comprehend the transformation that occurred at Ojai. Like the bewildered Nitya, we who are not able to come to these events through our own experience might naturally try to convey them using traditional vocabulary drawn from Yoga or Mahayana Buddhism. In the present context, however, it seems best to suspend judgement on the metaphysical significance of those events, and to focus on their import for Krishnamurti's life.

The 'process', as Nitya called it, occurred in phases spread over many months during 1922 and 1923. What seemed to be a physically painful ordeal was punctuated by visions of great beauty and moments of transparent clarity.

Very soon after reaching Ojai Valley, Krishnamurti began meditating steadily and easily. Then a pain developed along the nape of his neck, and over the next few weeks it grew more intense and shifted to different parts of his body. Mainly it was concentrated along the spine, behind the eyes and at the crown of his head.

Nitya watched his brother shudder, writhe in agony and often faint. He heard him speak in several voices. Sometimes he heard the voice of a nervous child expressing fear that 'Krishna' would go away and never return. On other occasions Nitya heard the voice of 'a protective stranger', and his notes record one side of a conversation 'with unseen forces'. At times Nitya heard these voices lapse into incoherence; at other times Krishnamurti seemed to be reliving past events. Nitya watched him revisit the scene of their mother's death, to see Narayaniah cover his face with his dhoti and weep. Then the voice became personal — a child lamenting in his long-forgotten mother tongue.

Krishnamurti could not explain what was happening to him; he often fell unconscious during the 'process' and did not recall afterwards what had occurred. But one clear record in his own words hints at how it transformed his consciousness. In a letter to Mrs Besant, he begins simply by saying: 'I had the most extraordinary experience.' The letter continues:

> There was a man mending the road; that man was myself; the pickaxe he held was myself; the very stone which he was breaking was a part of me; the tender blade of grass was my very being and the tree beside the man was myself. I almost could feel and think like the roadmender, and I could feel the wind passing through the tree and the little ant on the blade of grass I could feel. The birds, the dust and the very noise were a part of me... I was in everything, or rather everything was in me, inanimate and animate, the mountain, the worm and all breathing things.

This passage describes a personality dissolving in communion with what is 'out there'. A deep empathy, where subject and object blend, was an abiding part of Krishnamurti's character, already implicit in his childhood 'emptiness'. Between this inborn empathy and its full articulation in the statement 'You are the world', lay the development of Krishnamurti's mature insights. He had to learn why his own deep and abiding empathy was not an essential part of everyday human consciousness, and he had to discover an effective response to that fact. Krishnamurti's letter goes on to describe a pervasive tranquillity.

> Within myself was the calmness of the bottom of a deep and unfathomable lake. Like the lake I felt that my physical body with its mind and emotions could be ruffled on the surface, but nothing, nay nothing, could disturb the calmness of my soul.

There are indications of a growing confidence that in some sense he has lived up to Mrs Besant's expectations:

> I have seen the Light. I have touched compassion which heals all sorrow and suffering; it is not for myself, but for the world. . . Never can I be in darkness, I have seen the glorious and healing Light... I have drunk at the fountain of joy and eternal Beauty. I am God-intoxicated.

Around the same time he wrote an apologetic letter to CWL, pledging a renewed commitment to Theosophy and declaring that his future work lay in serving 'the Masters, and the Lord'.

In spite of this dutiful declaration, Krishnamurti never permitted his spiritual experience to form the keystone of any religious orthodoxy. Nor did he live with it as a dissonant memory, out of tune with daily life. Its residue in his consciousness was that 'silent space' in which all that was indifferent to truth could be held and examined, where all that was indifferent to love could be quenched. That silence found application in daily life, not in some other world; it fostered open understanding, not occult power.

Meanwhile the 'process', with its physical anguish, its dislocation of personality, its beatific visions and calm illuminations, continued over many months: across oceans and continents, as the brothers journeyed around the world. Nitya could not understand what was happening to his brother, nor did Krishnamurti himself comprehend the long-term implications of the changes that were taking place in his own consciousness. In Theosophical terms, their first thought was that the process might lead to expanded clairvoyance, or 'first-hand knowledge' of occult truths. But that did not come about. What did come about was a deepening of that 'silent space' which had now opened into an illumination that was not an event, but a state which Krishnamurti 'flowed into' naturally.

Dismayed by his brother's suffering, Nitya turned to Leadbeater for guidance — and found him curiously non-committal, even sceptical. From Australia, CWL wrote that Krishnamurti had now passed his 'third initiation', but that he himself had passed his fourth initiation earlier, with none of the physical side-effects of the Ojai 'process'. Troubled by these developments, perhaps suspecting that 'dark powers' might have seized his former protégé, CWL secretly dispatched one of his Theosophical physicians to Ojai for a report. Unfortunately no record of her report has survived.

❖

CWL published *The Masters and the Path* in 1925. The central metaphor of that book, the spiritual path, appears in many of the world's religions. One of its most beautiful realizations is found at the great Stupa of Borobudur, in which a gradually ascending physical path curves upward to symbolize the long spiritual path of life and rebirth. Sculptured friezes along this path illustrate Subandhu's long journey to enlightenment. In imitation of that ancient journey, pilgrims are drawn up to the summit by scenes from the life of Buddha and his many virtuous acts; and along the way they pass the figures of Bodhisattvas, their guides along the spiritual path of suffering and release.

Traditional Indian schools of thought can be classified according to whether they hold enlightenment to be sudden or gradual. Nagarjuna, on one side, was a 'leap' philosopher, whereas Patanjali's *Yoga Sutra* looks for enlightenment along a gradual path. The four stages of advancement recognized by Leadbeater locate his version of Theosophy somewhere between these two traditional alternatives.

The glimpse we catch of the young Krishnamurti in Europe, working closely with small groups in spiritual instruction, shows him already moving away from a 'path' toward a 'leap' philosophy better suited to his temperament and his understanding of the human condition. He exhorts his young disciples to value unselfishness, love and sympathy, to 'take a leap in the dark ... live dangerously ... it was 'so easy' and 'such fun to change'. Whereas Theosophy had promised an evolution of the spirit, Krishnamurti's teaching, even at this early period, aimed for something more like a revolution.

❖

A new generation of Theosophists was coming of age, eager to claim their places in the hierarchy. At a Star Camp at Huizen in Holland, George Arundale took the lead and during one momentous week in August 1925, 'brought down' a series of astral messages to advance himself and his associates along The Path. Hitherto only Mrs Besant and CWL had passed the 'Fourth Initiation'; now Arundale announced that he and his young wife Rukmini Devi had been granted that rank, along with Krishnamurti; and also that Lord Maitreya had chosen twelve Apostles and would reveal their names presently.

Mrs Besant, now almost seventy years old, was enthralled by the heady pace of these developments. At a Star Congress in Holland, she read out a list of seven Apostles: Wedgwood, Leadbeater, Jinarajadasa, Arundale, Rukmini Devi, Oscar Köllerström and herself. She added that in celebration of the Lord's Coming a World University would be established, with herself as Rector, Arundale as Principal and James Wedgwood as Director of Studies. Far away in Ojai, Krishnamurti was sceptical. He had been ministering to Nitya who was then very ill, and could not remember having participated in any of the reported events 'on the astral plane'. He would not confirm the advancement of Arundale and others, and he was not willing to accept them as Apostles.

❖

In November 1925, Nitya lost his battle with tuberculosis and died in Ojai. At that moment, Krishnamurti was on board ship en route to Adyar for the Golden Jubilee celebrations of the Theosophical Society. As they neared the Suez Canal telegrams arrived announcing Nitya's critical illness and later his death. Krishnamurti had agreed to attend the Golden Jubilee only after being persuaded that Nitya would be spared for his part in the work that lay ahead. In a dream earlier that year, Krishnamurti had pleaded for Nitya's life, and in that dream the Great Master Mahachohan had pronounced: 'He will live.' The mystical experiences of 1922 had drawn the brothers together in a common purpose, and in his innocence Krishnamurti accepted the promise made to him in a dream. His grief was now profound. He had loved Nitya with an ease born of common experience shared in perfect understanding. From childhood their lives had been intertwined; together they had shared the loss of family and loss of their own culture; together they had adjusted to alien surroundings. As his ship steamed towards Madras, Krishnamurti wrote a statement filled with a powerful sorrow whose quenching was to bring him new strength:

> An old dream is dead and a new one is being born. A new vision is coming into being and a new consciousness is being unfolded. I have wept, but I do not want others to weep.

B. Shiva Rao, who accompanied Krishnamurti on his fateful journey to Adyar, believed that Nitya's death marked the beginning of Krishnamurti's turning away from Theosophy:

> His entire philosophy of life — the implicit faith in the future as outlined by Mrs Besant and Mr Leadbeater, Nitya's vital part in it, were shattered.

While there is some truth in this — Nitya's death was undeniably a shattering event — Krishnamurti's dissatisfaction with Theosophy had been brewing for many years; and the events in Holland, followed by Nitya's death, had brought the matter to a crisis. In 1927 he would write:

> When I began to think for myself, which has been now for some years past, I found myself in revolt. I was not satisfied by any teaching, by any authority.

It was a revolt which had begun many years before Nitya's death, fueled by Krishnamurti's natural antipathy to authoritarianism, and by Leadbeater's firmly entrenched role as arbiter of spiritual advancement within the TS.

Nitya's death brought into focus Krishnamurti's dissatisfaction with Theosophy. When Mrs Besant tried to restore relations at Adyar, holding Krishnamurti's hand and once again asking him to accept Leadbeater, Arundale and others as Apostles, he refused for a second time. Later, under the shade of an old banyan tree at the Star Convention, Krishnamurti told his audience that the World Teacher would come only for 'those who want, who desire, who long'.

> For those who want sympathy, who want happiness, who are longing to be released, who are longing to find happiness in all things. . . I come not to destroy but to build.

In their excitement over the World Teacher's arrival, Krishnamurti's listeners would have been unaware that the teacher before them was suddenly addressing an entirely new set of concerns, and perhaps even actively seeking to create a new audience. Theosophists of the older generation, settled into their assigned places on The Path, were used to hearing reports about former lives and other worlds. Krishnamurti was now determined to focus on concerns of this life in this world, and to raise questions rather than give answers — a radical departure for which his listeners were unprepared.

Krishnamurti thus began to chart a clear course away from every aspect of Theosophical teaching. In his mature philosophy, in his talks, dialogues and writings, Krishnamurti found numerous ways of awakening the minds of his listeners. He advocated doubt and questioning as a method for spiritual enquiry:

> Doubt is a precious thing. It cleanses, purifies the mind. The very questioning, the very fact that the seed of doubt is in one, helps to clarify our investigations.

Opening of the heart, no less precious in this teaching, begins with a sense of beauty awakened by the wonders of life and the colours of nature, enjoyed in the presence of those 'who have drunk at the fountain'.

Opposition to Krishnamurti's new teachings soon arose within the TS and grew steadily. Mrs Besant made a valiant effort to build bridges between those teachings and the Master's Path of Discipleship. She even suspended the Esoteric Section, but Krishnamurti, now openly in revolt against all forms of spiritual authority, would not compromise for the sake of appearances. In 1929, at a Star Camp in Holland, he took the decisive step of disbanding the Order of the Star after proclaiming: 'Truth is a pathless land'.

❖

Krishnamurti's writings in the six years preceding 1929 reveal the searchlight turned inward, illuminating a maturing understanding. The earliest work called *The Path* was an inchoate, rambling prose-poem, rhapsodic and abstract, that described a weary seeker climbing an elusive path to perfection — alone, unaided, and burdened by many lives. Its fragmented and mutable protagonist subsumed within himself the many lives of Alcyone. Another semi-autobiographical piece called *The Search* had three figures:

'I', 'Thou' and 'The World' seeking redemption. The dominant theme and the tone of this writing can be seen in a stanza from *The Song of Life:*

> Caught in the agony of Time,
> Maimed by the inward stress of growth,
> O Beloved.
> The Self of which thou art the whole,
> Is seeking the way of illumined ecstasy.

He seemed to be laying Alcyone to rest when he declared in 1925 that 'Right thought and right deed in one life is more than a thousand incarnations of wasted lives.' After 1929 Alcyone's abstract voice and archaic vocabulary give way to an authentic teacher compassionately attentive to another human being's sorrow. A sense of particularity pervades these later encounters, even though they address universal human concerns. A silent space dissolves barriers between the participants and lends substance to Krishnamurti's saying: 'You are the world'.

Krishnamurti's mature teachings breathe new life into Buddha's precept: 'Be a light unto yourself'. For him those words hold one message for all human beings — question everything that governs the conduct of your life: examine your self-image, abandon your prejudice, attend to your relationships. And Krishnamurti did not hesitate to draw out the implication — that there can be no legitimate authorities in the spiritual life: no scriptures, no guru, no arbiter of spiritual advancement, no hierarchy. Each human being has to find freedom anew. The World Teacher was only a passer-by.

Krishnamurti extended his critique of spiritual evolution by questioning utopianism in the spiritual domain. In 1933 he cautioned his listeners against projecting distant 'ideals' in the vain hope of evolving into some better future, and requested them to resist the impulse to project his own teachings into a 'new ideal after which I must mould myself'. He knew that the projection of ideals was often a diversionary tactic, the mind's way of evading responsibility:

> If you are a prisoner, I am not concerned in describing what freedom is. My chief concern is to show what creates the prison and for *you* to break it down.

To break down the prison meant facing an often painful immediacy of 'what is' rather than chasing an often illusory promise of 'what should be' in some distant future.

❖

For the next fifty-five years after disbanding The Order of the Star in the East, Krishnamurti travelled to different parts of the world discoursing about his vision of life. The Foundations he established during these years served to organize his talks, publish his writings, run schools and offer facilities for study and meditation. He remained true to his sense that the individual was both the teacher and the taught — leaving no spiritual heirs, vesting no one with authority to judge another's religious standing.

Krishnamurti held that his teachings could become the basis for a new kind of education, and he established several schools in India, England and America. All these schools are located in beautiful landscapes and are dedicated to fostering a love of nature, concern for other human beings, and a questioning attitude to life.

According to Krishnamurti's own testimony, a key to understanding his development lies in the 'silent space' that was native to him. It was this space that freed him from the rigid orthodoxy into which he was born, that allowed him to emerge whole from his surrealistic upbringing within the TS and that helped him cope with failure as a student in England. Silence, at the heart of his teaching, dissolved boundaries.

> You are not an American, Russian, Hindu or Muslim. You are apart from these labels and words; you are the rest of mankind because your consciousness, your reactions, your faith, your beliefs, your ideologies, your fears, anxieties, loneliness, sorrow or pleasure, are similar to the rest of mankind. If you change, it will affect the rest of mankind.

That silent space, nourished and replenished over many years, became a vast expanse flowing through his long life.

❖

The idea of progress, so deeply entrenched in nineteenth century thought, stretched Darwinian evolution far beyond its home ground in biology, and made it one of the guiding metaphors of the age. It was widely held to confirm a now discredited claim for human supremacy over the rest of nature, and was later enlisted in service of the notorious doctrine of a master race. For social reformers on the political left it helped inspire utopian ideals of communism, and on the political right it gave comfort to ideologues who found 'survival of the fittest' a convenient excuse for inequities in the status quo. Theosophy as known to Krishnamurti and within which he lived his formative years had carried the notion of evolutionary progress to its farthest extreme by looking for spiritual advancement above and beyond the human condition, in a mythical future 'root race'.

By now, at the end of the twentieth century, the idea of evolutionary progress is completely played out. In the unabashed words of Stephen Jay Gould, a leading evolutionary biologist:

> Progress is a noxious, culturally embedded, untenable, non-operational, intractable idea that must be replaced if we wish to understand the pattern of history.

Krishnamurti's critique of evolutionary progress in the spiritual realm was vigorous, sustained and thorough. It was based on first hand observation of the human condition, long before the limits of evolutionary progress were understood in biology, social reform and political economy. It loomed large in Krishnamurti's revolt against his Theosophical upbringing, and became an enduring part of his philosophy of life.

Radhika Herzberger

Notes

Pages 9-1 0: For overviews of the early colonial period in India see TREVELYAN and KOPF. Details of the debate between proponents of English and the Orientalists are provided in EMBREE. A full discussion of the concept of progress can be found in BURY. 'The British had nothing to give...' is from TREVELYAN (45), and 'Not in vain the distance beacons . . . ' is from Tennyson's *Locksley Hall*.

Pages 11 -13: Several details of Krishnamurti's early life have been draw from J.KRISHNAMURTI 1913, an 'autobiography' written at the age of eighteen. A typescript of this piece, barely six pages in length, was found in the papers and documents left by B. Shiva Rao, along with a document dictated by Krishnamurti's father, which gives a moving account of Krishnamurti's childhood as part of an orthodox Telugu Brahmin family. BALFOUR CLARKE is an additional primary source containing recollections of Dick Clarke's years as tutor to Krishnamurti and Nityananda during this period.

Page 14: The quotations are from LEADBEATER (45). Additional material on Madame Blavatsky has been derived from MEADE.

Page 16: TAYLOR offers an exhaustive survey of the many stages in Mrs. Besant's varied political life, and WESSINGER is a good source for her religious ideas.

Page 17: TILLETT carefully traces the entanglement of fact and fiction in Leadbeater's personal history. The passage concerning Lord Krishna's incarnation is from *Bhagavad Gita* IV.7.

Pages 18-19: B. Shiva Rao's unpublished notes of these early events in Krishnamurti's life are important sources, on which LUTYENS and JAYAKAR have based some of their history of this period.

Pages 20-21: Krishnamurti's description of his fourteen-year old self was narrated to me by Dr S. Balasundaram, who was present on the occasion. Similar statements by Krishnamurti appear in KRISHNAMURTI 1987, 1990. He talked at length about CWL with Trustees of the Krishnamurti Foundation of America at Ojai in 1972. The shock of being struck by CWL seems to have destroyed Krishnamurti's respect for him, and the affection which Krishnamurti felt for CWL seems to have gradually declined over a long period of time, finally turning to disdain. See TILLETT (10). Extended coverage of Narayaniah's court case may be found in NETHERCOT. For a sampling of Mrs. Besant's affectionate letters to Krishnamurti see JAYAKAR.

Page 22: The nineteenth century produced other charismatic figures with a similar penchant for re-creating their own lives. The British explorer Stanley, born as John Rowlands in 1844, took on a new name and a whole new family background along with a colourful *persona* he invented for himself to embellish his search for the source of the Nile. Audubon, the most famous naturalist of his times, was born of a Creole mother and a French sea captain, but preferred his American compatriots to believe that he was the Lost Dauphin of France.

Page 23: In his autobiography, Leonard Woolf re-creates the atmosphere of England before the First World War; the words on truth and beauty are from WOOLF (20).

Page 25: Dick Clarke, who assisted Arundale as Krishnamurti's tutor during these years, observed a 'spirit of unspoken revolt' growing in him as early as 1912, when Krishnamurti was put through a daily routine of 'magnetizing' hundreds of blue ribbons and silver stars for members of the Order of the Star; see BALFOUR-CLARKE (34). Krishnamurti's letters are drawn from LUTYENS (Ch. 13).

Page 26: On Krishnamurti's last meeting with his father see KRISHNAMURTI 1982, (36f) for his own later recollection of the incident and JAYAKAR (43f) for the very different recollection of Narayaniah's daughter-in-law, who was also present on that occasion.

Pages 27-28: The 'process' is described at length in LUTYENS and in JAYAKAR. For Krishnamurti's letter to Mrs Besant see JAYAKAR (47f).

Page 29: For the exchange between Krishnamurti and Leadbeater see LUTYENS (163).

Pages30-31: The terminology of 'gradual' and 'leap' philosophy is due to POTTER, which develops this classification in detail. Krishnamurti's advice to take 'a leap in the dark' is from LUTYENS (77). Different aspects of the events at Huizen in Holland are covered in NETHERCOT, LUTYENS and TILLETT.

Page 32: Krishnamurti described his dream about the Mahachohan in a letter to Mrs Besant from Adyar on February 10, 1925; see JAYAKAR.

Page 33: 'When I began to think for myself...' is from KRISHNAMURTI 1927 (1). 'For those who want sympathy...' is from *The Herald of the Star*, 1926.

Page 34: 'Doubt is a precious thing...' comes from KRISHNAMURTI 1988 (25).

Pages 34-35: The *Path, The Search* and *The Song of Life* are published in KRISHNAMURTI 1981.

Page 36: 'If you are a prisoner...' is from KRISHNAMURTI 1991(53).

Page 37: 'You are not an American, Russian ...' is from KRISHNAMURTI 1988 (61).

Page 37: Among Gould's numerous books on evolutionary biology, paleontology and history of science is GOULD, an extended critique of the notion of evolutionary progress.

Bibliography

BALFOUR-CLARKE, RUSSELL. *The Boyhood of J. Krishnamurti.* Bombay: Chetana, 1977.

BURY, JOHN. *The Idea of Progress.* New York: Dover, 1955.

EMBREE, AINLEE. *India's Search For National Identity.* New Delhi: Chanakya, 1980.

GOULD, STEPHEN JAY. *Wonderful Life.* London: Penguin Books, 1989.

JAYAKAR, PUPUL. Krishnamurti, *A Biography.* New York: Harper and Row, 1986.

KOPF, DAVID. *The Brahmo Samaj and the Shaping of the Modern Indian Mind.* Princeton University Press, 1979.

KRISHNAMURTI, J. [1911] *At the Feet of the Master.* Madras: Theosophical Publishing House, 1911.

— [1913] *Fifty Years of My Life.* Unpublished typescript.

— [1926] *Towards Discipleship.* Madras: Theosophical Publishing House.

— [1927] *Who Brings the Truth?* The Star Publishing Trust.

— [1961] *Commentaries on Living, Third Series.* London: Victor Gollancz.

— [1981] *Poems and Parables.* London: Victor Gollancz.

— [1982] *Krishnamurti's Journal.* London: Victor Gollancz.

— [1988] *Krishnamurti to Himself: His Last Journal.* London: Victor Gollancz.

— [1990] *Tradition and Revolution.* 2nd ed. Madras : KFI Publications.

— [1991] *Collected Works, Volume I.* Dubuque, Iowa: Kendall Hunt.

LEADBEATER, C.W. *The Masters and the Path,* 3rd ed. Madras: The Theosophical Publishing House, 1992.

LUTYENS, MARY. *Krishnamurti: The Years of Awakening.* London: John Murray, 1975.

MEADE, MARION. *Madame Blavatsky, The Woman Behind the Myth.* New York: Putnam, 1980.

NETHERCOT, ARTHUR H. *The Last Four Lives of Annie Besant.* London: Rupert Hart-Davis, 1963.

POTTER, KARL. *Presuppositions of India's Philosophies.* Prentice Hall, Englewood, New Jersey: 1963.

TAYLOR, ANNE. *Annie Besant, A Biography.* Oxford: Oxford University Press, 1992.

THOMSON, DAVID. *Nineteenth Century England.* London: Penguin, 1950.

TILLETT, GREGORY. *The Elder Brother, A Biography of Charles Webster Leadbeater.* London: Routledge & Kegan Paul, 1982.

TREVELYAN, RALEIGH. *The Golden Oriole.* New York: Viking, 1987.

WESSINGER, CATHERINE KNOWMAN. *Annie Besant and Progressive Messianism. Studies in Women and Religion,* Vol. 26. Lewiston, New York: The Edwin Mellen Press, 1989.

WOOLF, LEONARD. *An Autobiography, 2:1911-1969.* Oxford: Oxford University Press: 1980.

I

Public Talks

Thought Breeds Fear

It seems to me that it is always good to be serious, especially when we are sitting down here talking about serious things. We need a certain attention, a certain quality of penetration, and a deep enquiry into the various problems that each one of us has and into the problems that the world is facing. As one observes, not only in this country, but right throughout the world, there is chaos, a great deal of confusion and human misery in ev revolt going on there among the young; they no longer accept the tradition, the authority, the pattern of society.

And when one comes to this country, as we do every year, one sees the rapid decline, the poverty, the utter disregard for human beings, the political chicanery, the absolute cessation of any religious, deep enquiry, the tribal warfare between various groups, and fasting over some trivial affair. When the house is burning, when there is such chaos, when there is such misery, to spend one's life or even make an exhibition of oneself over some trivial affair indicates the state of mind of those who are supposed to be leaders, religious or political.

When one observes all these facts, not only outwardly, organizationally, economically, socially, but also inwardly, apart from all the repetition of traditions, apart from the accepted norms of thought and the innumerable platitudes that one utters, and when one goes deeply beyond all this inwardly, one will find that there is also great chaos, contradiction.

One does not know what to do. One is always seeking endlessly, going from one book to another, from one philosophy to another, from one teacher to another. And what we are really seeking is not clarity, is not the understanding of the actual state of mind, but rather we are searching for ways and means to escape from ourselves. Religions in different forms throughout the world have offered this escape, and we are satisfied in trying to find out a convenient, pleasurable, satisfying retreat. When one observes all this — the increasing population, the utter callousness of human beings, the utter disregard for others' feelings, for others' lives, the utter neglect of the social structure — one wonders if order out of this chaos can be brought about. Not political order — politics can never bring about order; neither an economic structure nor a different ideology can bring about order. But we do need order. For there is a great deal of disorder, both outwardly and inwardly, of which one is vaguely, speculatively, casually aware. One feels the problems are too immense. The population is exploding so fast that one asks oneself, 'What can I do as a human being living in this chaotic misery, violence, stupidity? What can I do?' Surely, you must have asked this question of yourself if you are at all serious. And if one has asked oneself this very serious question, 'What can one do oneself?' the invariable answer is, 'I am afraid I can do very little to alter the structure of society, to bring about order, not only within, but also outwardly.'

And generally one asks the question, 'What can I do?' and invariably the answer is 'very little'. There one stops. But the problem demands a much deeper answer. The challenge is so great that every one of us must respond to it totally, not with some conditioned reply — not as a Hindu, as a Buddhist, as a Muslim, as a Parsi, as a Christian; all these are dead, gone, finished; they have no longer any meaning except for the politician who exploits ignorance and superstition. The scriptures, what has been said by the philosophers, by the authorities in religion with their sanctions and with their demands that you obey, that you follow — these have totally lost all meaning for any man who is aware, who is conscious of the problems of the world.

You know, man has lost faith in what he has believed; he no longer follows anybody. You understand what is happening politically when the audience throws shoes and stones at the speaker? It means that they are discarding leadership. They do not want to be told what to do any more. Man is in despair. Man is in confusion. There is a great deal of sorrow. And no ideology, whether of the left or the right, has any meaning. All ideologies are idiotic anyhow. They have no meaning when they are faced with the actual fact of 'what is'. So we can disregard not only the authority of leadership but also the authority of the priest, the authority of the book, the authority of religion. We can totally disregard all these, and we have to disregard them in order to find out what is true. Nor can you go back to what has been. You know, one hears often in this country about the heritage of India, what India has been. They are everlastingly talking about the past, what India was. And the people who generally talk about the cultures of the past have very little thought; they can repeat what has been, what the books have said, and it is a convenient dope with which to lull the people. So we can disregard all those, sweep them completely away; we have to because we have problems that demand tremendous attention, deep thought, and enquiry, not a repetition of what somebody has said, however great he may be. So when you put away all the things that have been, that have brought about this immense misery, this utter brutality and violence, then we are confronted with facts, actually with 'what is', both outwardly and inwardly, not with 'what should be'. The 'what should be' has no meaning.

You know, revolutions — like the French Revolution, the Russian Revolution, the Communist Revolution — have been made on ideologies of 'what should be'. And after killing millions and millions of people, they are discovering that people are tired of ideologies. So you are no longer ideologists, no longer leaders; you have no longer anybody to tell you what to do. You are now facing the world by yourself, alone, and you have to act. So our problem becomes immensely great, frightening. You, as a human being, alone, without any support from anybody, have to think out the problems clearly, and act without any confusion so that you become an oasis in a desert of ideas. Do you know what an oasis is? It is a place with a few trees, water, and a little pasturage in a vast desert where there is nothing but sand and confusion. That is what each one of us has to be at the present time — an oasis, where we are — so that each one of us is free, clear, not confused, and can act, not according to personal inclination or according to one's temperament or compelled by circumstances.

So the challenge is very great, and you cannot reply to it by running away from it. It is at your door. So you have got to take stock. You have got to look around. You have got to find out what to do for yourself. And that is what we are going to do together. The speaker is not going to tell you what to do because there is, for him, no authority. And this is very important for you to understand — that all spiritual authority has come to an end because it has led to confusion, to endless misery, to conflict. It is only the most foolish that follow.

So if we can put aside all authority, then we can begin to investigate, to explore. And to explore you must have energy, not only physical energy, but mental energy, where the brain functions actively, not made dull by repetition. It is only when there is friction that energy is wasted. Please follow this a little bit. Don't accept what the speaker says, because that has no meaning. We are concerned with freedom, not a particular kind of freedom, but the total freedom of man. So we need energy, not only to bring about a great psychological, spiritual revolution in ourselves, but also to investigate, to look, to act. And as long as there is friction of any kind, friction in relationship between husband and wife, between man and man, between one community and another community, between one country and another country, outwardly or inwardly, as long as there is conflict in any form, however subtle it may be, there is a wastage of energy. And there is the summit of energy when there is freedom.

Now we are going to enquire and discover for ourselves how to be free from this friction, from this conflict. You and I are going to take a journey into it, exploring, enquiring, asking — never following. Therefore, to enquire there must be freedom. And there is no freedom when there is fear. We are burdened with fear, not only outwardly, but inwardly. There is the outward fear of losing a job, of not having enough food to eat, of losing your position, of your boss behaving in an ugly manner. Inwardly also there is a great deal of fear — the fear of not being, of not becoming a success; the fear of death; the fear of loneliness; the fear of not being loved; the fear of utter boredom, and so on. So there is this fear, and it is this fear that prevents the enquiry into all the problems and being free from them. It is this fear that prevents a deep enquiry within ourselves.

So our first problem, our really essential problem, is to be free from fear. You know what fear does? It darkens the mind. It makes the mind dull. From fear there is violence. From fear there is this worship of something which you know nothing about; therefore you invent ideas, images — images made by the hand or by the mind and various philosophies. And the more you are clever, the more you have authority in your voice and in your gesture, the more the ignorant follow you. So our first concern is: Is it possible to be totally free from fear? Please put that question to yourselves and find out.

During these four talks, what you are trying to do is to bring about an action on the part of a human being in a world that is a desert, that is in confusion, that is of violence, so that each one of us becomes an oasis. And to discover that and to bring about that clarity, that precision, so that the mind is capable of going far beyond all thought, there must be, first, freedom from all fear.

Now, first, there is the physical fear that is the animal response. Because we have inherited a great deal of the animal; a great part of our brain structure is the heritage of the animal. That is a scientific fact. It is not a theory, it is a fact. The animals are violent, so are human beings. The animals are greedy; they love to be flattered, they love to be petted; they like to find comfort; so do human beings. The animals are acquisitive, competitive; so are human beings. The animals live in groups; so do human beings like to function in groups. The animals have a social structure; so have human beings. We can go on much more in detail. But it is sufficient to see that there is a great deal in us which is still of the animal.

And is it possible for us not only to be free of the animal but also to go far beyond that and find out — not merely enquire verbally, but actually find out — whether the mind can go beyond the conditioning of a society, of a culture in which it is brought up? To discover, or to come upon, something which is totally of a different dimension, there must be freedom from fear.

Obviously, self-protective reaction is not fear. We need food, clothes, and shelter — all of us, not only the rich, not only the high. Everybody needs them, and this cannot be solved by politicians. The politicians have divided the world into countries, like India, each with its separate sovereign government, with its separate army, and all this poisonous nonsense about nationalism. There is only one political problem, and that is to bring about human unity. And that cannot be brought about if you cling to your nationality, to your trivial divisions as the South, the North, the Telugu, the Tamil, the Gujarati, and what not — it all becomes so infantile. When the house is burning, sir, you don't talk about the man who is bringing the water, you do not talk about the colour of the hair of the man who set the house on fire, but you bring water. Nationalism has divided man as religions have divided man, and this nationalist spirit and the religious beliefs have separated man, put man against man. And one can see why it has come into being. It is because we all like to live in a little puddle of our own.

And so one has to be free from fear, and that is one of the most difficult things to do. Most of us are not aware that we are afraid, and we are not aware of what we are afraid. And when we know of what we are afraid, we do not know what to do. So we run away from it. You understand, sir? We run away from what we are, which is fear; and what we run away to increases fear. And we have developed, unfortunately, a network of escapes. So one has to become aware not only of the fears one has but also of the network which one has developed and through which one runs away.

Now, how does fear come into being? You are afraid of something — afraid of death, afraid of your wife, husband; afraid of losing a job, afraid of so many things. Now take one particular fear that you have and become conscious of it. We will proceed to examine how it comes into being and what we can do about it, how to resolve it completely. Then we shall establish a right relationship between you and the speaker. This is not mass psychology, or mass self-psychoanalysis, but an enquiry into certain facts which we have to face together. How does fear come about — fear of tomorrow, fear of losing a job, fear of death, fear of falling ill, fear of pain? Fear implies a process of thought about the future or about the past. I am afraid of tomorrow, of what might happen. I am afraid of death; it is at a distance still, but I am afraid of it. Now, what brings about fear? Fear always exists in relation to something. Otherwise there is no fear. So one is afraid of tomorrow or of what has been or what will be. What has brought fear? Isn't it thought? I think that I might lose my job tomorrow; therefore I am afraid. I might die, and I do not want to die; I have lived a wretched, monstrous, ugly, brutal, insensitive life without any feeling, and yet I do not want to die; and thought creates the future as death, and I am frightened of that.

Do you follow all this? Please, do not merely accept words. Don't merely listen to certain words. But rather listen because it is your problem. It is your everyday problem, whether you are asleep or awake — this matter of fear. You have to solve it yourself; nobody is going to solve it for you. No mantras, no meditation, no god, no priest, no government, no analyst, nobody is going to solve it for you. So you have to understand it, you have to go beyond it. Therefore please listen. Not with your cunning mind; don't say, 'I will listen and compare what he says with what I already know, or with what has been said' — then you are not listening. To listen you must give your complete attention. To give complete attention means care. There can be only attention when you have affection, when you have love, which means that you want to resolve this problem of fear. When you have resolved it, you become a human being, a free man who can create an oasis in a world that is decaying.

So thought breeds fear. I think about my losing a job or I might lose a job, and thought creates the fear. So thought always projects itself in time, because thought is time. I think about the illness I have had and I do not like pain, and I am frightened that the pain might return again. I have had an experience of pain; thinking about it and not wanting it create fear. Fear is very closely related to pleasure. Most of us are guided by pleasure. To us, like the animals, pleasure is of the highest importance, and pleasure is part of thought. By thinking about something that has given me pleasure, that pleasure is increased. Isn't it? Have you not noticed all this? You have had an experience of pleasure —

of a beautiful sunset or of sex — and you think about it. The thinking about it increases pleasure, as thinking about what you have had as pain brings fear. So thought creates pleasure and fear. Doesn't it? So thought is responsible for the demand for and the continuation of pleasure; and thought is also responsible for engendering fear, bringing about fear. One sees this; this is an actual experimental fact.

Then one asks oneself, 'Is it possible not to think about pleasure or pain? Is it possible to think only when thought is demanded, but not otherwise?' Sir, when you function in an office, when you are working at a job, thought is necessary; otherwise, you could not do anything. When you speak, when you write, when you talk, when you go to the office, thought is necessary. There it must function precisely, impersonally. There thought must not be guided by inclination, a tendency. There thought is necessary. But is thought necessary in any other field of action?

Please follow this. For us thought is very important; that is the only instrument we have. Thought is the response of memory which has been accumulated through experience, through knowledge, through tradition; and memory is the result of time, inherited from the animal. And with this background we react. This reaction is thinking. Thought is essential at certain levels. But when thought projects itself as the future and the past psychologically, then thought creates fear as well as pleasure; and in this process the mind is made dull and therefore inaction is inevitable. Sir, fear, as we said, is brought about by thought — thinking about losing my job, thinking my wife might run away with somebody, thinking about death, thinking about what has been, and so on. Can thought stop thinking about the past psychologically, self-protectively, or about the future?

You understand the question? You see, sir, the mind, in which is included the brain, can invent and can overcome fear. To overcome fear is to suppress it, to discipline it, to control it, to translate it in terms of something else; but all that implies friction, doesn't it? When I am afraid, I say to myself, 'I must control it, I must run away from it, I must go beyond it' — all that implies conflict, doesn't it? And that conflict is a waste of energy. But if I understood how fear comes into being, then I could deal with it. I see how thought creates fear. So I ask myself, 'Is it possible for thought to stop, as otherwise fear will go on?' Then I ask myself, 'Why do I think about the future? Why do I think about tomorrow?' or 'Why do I think about what has been as pain or pleasure yesterday?'

Please listen quietly; we know that thought creates fear. One of the functions of thought is to be occupied, to be thinking about something all the time. Like a housewife who thinks about the food, the children, the washing up — that is all her occupation; remove that occupation, and she will be lost, she will feel totally uncomfortable, lonely, miserable. Or take away the God from the man who worships God, who is occupied with God; he will be totally lost. So thought must be occupied with something or the other, either about itself or about politics, or about how to bring about a different world, a different ideology, and so on; the mind must be occupied. And most of us want to be occupied; otherwise we shall feel lost; otherwise we do not know what to do, we will be lonely, we will be confronted with what we actually are. You understand? So you are occupied, thought is occupied — which prevents you from looking at yourself, at what you actually are.

We are concerned with bringing about a different world, a different social order. We are concerned not with religious beliefs and dogmas, superstitions, and rituals but with what is true religion. And to find that out there must be no fear. We see that thought breeds fear, and that thought must be occupied with something, as otherwise it feels itself lost. One of the reasons why we are occupied with God, with social reform, with this, with that, or with something or the other is because in ourselves we are afraid to be lonely, in ourselves we are afraid to be empty. We know what the world is: a world of brutality, ugliness, violence, wars, hatreds, class and national divisions, and so on. Knowing actually what the world is — not what we think it should be — our concern is to bring about a radical transformation in that. To bring about that transformation, the human mind has to undergo tremendous mutation; and the transformation cannot take place if there is any form of fear.

Therefore one asks oneself, 'Is it possible for thought to come to an end so that one lives completely, fully?' Have you ever noticed that when you attend completely, when you give your attention completely to anything, there is no observer and therefore no thinker, there is no centre from which you are observing? Do it sometime, give your attention completely — not 'concentration'. Concentration is the most absurd form of thought; that any schoolboy can do. What we are talking about is 'attention' — that is, to give attention. If you are listening now with all your being, with your mind, with your brain, with your nerves, with your total energy — listening; not accepting, not contradicting, not comparing, but actually listening with complete attention — is there an entity who is listening, who is observing? You will find that there is no observer at all. Now, when you look at a tree, look with complete attention. There are so many trees here, look at them. When you listen to the sound of the crows going to bed at night, listen to it completely. Don't say, 'I like that sound', or 'I don't like that sound'. Listen to it with your heart, with your mind, with your brain, with your nerves, completely. So also see the tree without the interference of thought — which means no space between the observer and the observed. When you give such total and complete attention, there is no observer at all. And it is the observer that breeds fear because the observer is the centre of thought; it is the 'me', the 'I', the self, the ego; the observer is the censor. When there is no thought, there is no observer. That state is not a blank state. That demands a great deal of enquiry — never accepting anything.

You know, you have accepted all your life; you have accepted tradition, you have accepted the family, you have accepted society as it is. You are merely an entity who says yes. You never say no to any of these things; and when you do say no, it is merely a revolt. And revolt creates its own pattern which then becomes habit, tradition. But if you have understood the whole social structure, you will see that it is based on conflict, on competition, and on the ruthless assertion of oneself at any price, either in the name of God or in the name of the country, in the name of peace, and so on.

So to be free of fear, give complete attention. Next time fear arises in your mind — fear of what is going to happen, or fear that something that has happened might come back again — give your complete attention; do not run away from it, don't try to change it, don't try to control it, don't try to suppress it, be with it totally, completely, with complete attention. Then you will see that because there is no observer there is no fear at all.

One of our peculiar fallacies is that we think there is the unconscious, a deep-rooted thing which is going to bring fear in different forms. You understand? All consciousness has its limitations. And to go beyond the limited conscious, conditioned entity, it is no good dividing it as the 'conscious' and the 'unconscious'. There is only the conscious field; and if you give attention at any moment completely, then you will wipe away the unconscious as well as the limited consciousness.

Attention cannot be cultivated. There is no method, no system, no practice by which you can have attention. Because when you practise a method to become attentive, it shows that you are cultivating inattention; what you are concerned with, then, is to cultivate attention through being inattentive. When you follow a system, a method, what are you doing? You are cultivating mechanically certain habits, repeating a certain activity which only dulls the mind; it does not sharpen the mind. Whereas if you give attention even for a second or a minute, completely, then you will see that momentary total attention wipes away that which you have been afraid of. In that attention there is neither the observer nor the observed. The observer then is the observed. But to understand that, to go into that, one has to enquire into the whole problem of time and space.

But, you see, our difficulty is we are so heavily conditioned that we never look, never ask, never question, never doubt. We are all followers, we are all yes-sayers. And the present crisis demands that you do not follow anybody. You, out of your confusion, cannot follow anybody, for when you are confused and you follow somebody, you are following out of confusion, not out of clarity. If you are clear, you will never follow anybody. And when you follow somebody out of your confusion, you will create more confusion. So what you have to do is to stop first, enquire, look, listen.

Unfortunately, this country is very old in its so-called culture. 'Culture' is a very good word, but it has been spoiled by the politicians, by the people who have very little thought, or very little of something original to say. So they have used this word 'culture' to cover up their own thoughtlessness. But to bring about a different culture — which means to grow, to flower, not to remain in a static state — and to understand that, one has to begin with oneself. Because, you are the result of this culture, the culture of India, with all the traditions, with all the superstitions, with all the fears, the culture in which there is religion, social divisions, linguistic divisions. You are a part of all that, you are that; you are not separate from that. So the moment you are aware of and give your total attention to what you are, then you will see that you have dropped all that instantly. Then you are free from the past completely. It is only when you are aware of your conditioning that it falls away from you naturally — not through any volition, not through any habit, not through any reaction; but it just drops away because you are giving your attention.

But most of us walk through life inattentively. We are rarely attentive. And when we are attentive, generally we react according to our conditioning as a Hindu, a Buddhist, a communist, a socialist, or what you will. And therefore we answer from the background in which we have been brought up. Therefore such reaction only creates further bondage, further conditioning. But when you become aware of your conditioning — just be aware, just give a little attention — then you will see that your mind is no longer divided as the conscious and the unconscious; then you will see that your mind is no longer chattering endlessly. Therefore the mind becomes extraordinarily sensitive. And it is only a very sensitive mind that can be silent — not a brutalized mind, not a mind that has been tortured through discipline, control, adjustment, or conformity; such a mind can never be quiet through repetition which it calls meditation. Meditation is something entirely different — a subject which we will perhaps go into another time.

As we said, a mind that is afraid, do what it will, will have no love whatsoever; and without love you cannot construct a new world. Without love there can be no oasis. And you, as a human being, have created this social structure in which you are caught. To break away from that — and you have to break from it completely — you have to understand yourself, just to observe yourself as you actually are. Then out of that clarity comes action. And then you will find out for yourself a different way of living, a way of life which is not repetitive, which is not conforming, which is not imitating, a life which is really free and therefore a life that opens the door to something which is beyond all thought.

The Collected Works of J.Krishnamurti: vol. XVII
First Talk in Bombay, 1967

Freedom, Relationship and Death

If we may, we will continue with what we were talking about the other day when we met here. We were saying that a radical revolution is necessary, a revolution that is not merely economic or social but at much greater depth, at the very root of consciousness. We were saying that not only do the world conditions demand that this revolution take place but also throughout the world there is a steady decline, not technologically, but in a sense religiously, if I may use that word cautiously and with a great deal of hesitancy. Because the word 'religion' has been so thoroughly misused; the intellectual people discard it totally, they deny it, they run away from that word; the scientists, the intellectuals, even the humanitarians, will have nothing to do with that word, with that feeling, or with those organized beliefs which are called religion. But we are talking of a revolution in the very nature of the psyche itself, in the very structure of consciousness that has been put together through millennia, through many, many experiences, through many conditions.

We are going into this question: whether it is possible for a human being living in this world — in this brutal, violent, rather ruthless world that is becoming more and more efficient and therefore more and more ruthless — to bring about a revolution, not only outwardly in his social relationship, but also much more in his inward life. It seems to me that unless there is a fundamental revolution in the whole of consciousness — that is, in the whole field of thinking — man will not only deteriorate and so perpetuate violence, sorrow, but also create a society that will become more and more mechanical, more and more pleasure giving, and therefore he will lead a very, very superficial life. If one observes, that is what is actually taking place.

Man is having more and more leisure through automation, through the development of cybernetics, through electronic brains, and so on. And that leisure is going to be used either for entertainment — religious entertainment, or entertainment through various forms of amusements — or for more and more destructive purposes in relationship between man and man; or, having that leisure, he is going to turn inwardly. There are only these three possibilities. Technologically he can go to the moon, but that will not solve the human problem. Nor will the mere use of his leisure for a religious or some other amusement solve it. Going to church or temple, beliefs, dogmas, reading sacred books — all that is really a form of amusement. Or man will go deeply into himself and question every value that man has created through the centuries, and try to find out if there is something more than the mere product of the brain. There are whole groups of people, throughout the world, that are revolting against the established order by taking various forms of drugs, denying any form of activity in society and so on.

So what we are talking about is whether it is possible for man living in this world to bring about a revolution, a psychological revolution which will create a different kind of society, a different kind of order. We need order, for there is a great deal of disorder. The whole social structure, as it is, is based on disorder, competition, rivalry, dog eating dog, man against man, class divisions, racial divisions, national divisions, tribal divisions, and so on, so that in the society as it is constructed there is disorder. There is no question about it. Various forms of revolution — the Russian and other forms of revolution — have tried to bring about order in society and they have invariably failed, as is shown in Russia and in China. But we need order because without order we cannot live. Even animals demand order. Their order is the order of property and sexual order. And also with us, human beings, it is the same order in property and sexual order — and we are willing to give up sexual order for rights over property; and in this field we are trying to bring about order.

Now, there can be order only when there is freedom — not as it is interpreted. Where there is no freedom, there is disorder, and therefore there is tyranny, and there are ideologies imposed upon man to bring about order which ultimately bring about disorder. So order implies discipline. But discipline, as is generally understood, is the discipline based on conformity, on obedience, on acceptance, or brought about through fear, through punishment, through a great deal of tyrannical power to keep you in order. We are talking of a discipline that comes through the very understanding of what freedom is. The understanding of what freedom is brings about its own discipline.

So we have to comprehend what we mean by these two words 'freedom' and 'understanding'. Generally we say, I understand something — that is intellectually, verbally. When anything is clearly stated either in your own language or in a foreign language which we both understand, then you say, 'I understand'. That is, only a part of the human totality is used when you say, 'I understand'. That is to say, you understand the words intellectually, you understand what the speaker means. But we do not mean, when we use the word 'understand', an intellectual comprehension of a concept. We are using that word 'understand' totally — that is, when you understand something, you act. When you understand that there is some danger, when you see a danger very clearly, there is immediate action. The action of understanding is its own discipline. So one has to grasp the significance of this word 'understand' very clearly. When we understand, realize, comprehend, see the thing as it is, there is action. And to understand something, you have to apply not only your mind, your reason, your capacity, but also your total attention; otherwise there is no understanding. I think that is fairly clear.

So we are seeing that the understanding of freedom is entirely different from revolt. A revolt is a reaction against the established order — like the revolt of the people who grow long hair and so on. They are revolting against the set pattern; but when they revolt, they accept the pattern in which they are caught. We are talking of freedom which is not a revolt. It is not a freedom from something but a freedom which is in the very understanding of disorder. Please follow this clearly. In the very understanding of what is disorder, there comes freedom which brings about order, in which there is discipline.

That is, to understand negatively is to bring about a positive act. Not through pursuing a positive pattern will order come. There is disorder. This disorder is caused by man pursuing a certain pattern — a social pattern, an ethical pattern, a religious pattern, a pattern which is based on his own personal inclination or pleasure, and so on. That is, this society is built on an acquisitive approach of life, on competitiveness, on obedience, on authority — which has brought about disorder. Each man is out for himself. The religious man is out for himself; the politician is out for himself, though he talks about 'for the good of the country'; and the businessman is out for himself. Each man is out for himself — that is obvious. And therefore he creates disorder. There are ideologists who say that man is working for himself, and therefore he must work for the country, for society as a community, and so on. Therefore order is imposed upon us — which brings disorder. This is fairly obvious, historically. So in understanding disorder — how each human being creates disorder — not verbally, not intellectually, but actually, in seeing actually the fact of what he is doing, then out of that perception, out of that observation of actually 'what is', and in the understanding of that, there is a discipline which brings about order.

So we have to understand, comprehend the word 'freedom', the word 'understand', and also the word 'see'. Do we see anything, or do we see it through the image which we have about that thing? When you look at a tree, you are looking at the actual fact of the tree through the image you have about the tree. Please observe it yourself, watch yourself. How do you look at the tree? Do it now, as we are talking. You look at it with thought; you say, 'It is a palm tree; it is this tree or that tree'. The thought prevents you from looking at the actual fact of that tree. Move a little more subjectively, more inwardly. You look at your wife or your husband through the image you have created about that person. Obviously, because you have lived with her or with him for many years, and you have cultivated an image about her or him. So you look at her or him through the image you have, and the relationship is between the two images that you have cultivated — not between two human beings. So you do not actually see, but one image is seeing the other image.

And this is very important to realize because we are dealing with human relationships throughout the world. As long as these images remain, there is no relationship; hence the whole conflict between man and man. It is an actual fact that each one of us is creating an image about the other, and that when we look at the other, we are looking at the image we have about him or he has about us. You have to see this fact. To see is different from verbalizing about it. When you are hungry, you know it. Nobody needs to tell you that you are hungry. Now, if somebody were to tell you that you are hungry, and you accept that statement, it has quite a different significance other than your being actually hungry. Now, in the same way, you have actually to realize that you have an image about another, and that when you look at another as a Hindu, as a Muslim, as a communist, and so on, all human relationship ceases, and you are only looking at the opinion you have created about another.

So we are asking whether it is at all possible to bring about a revolution in this image-making. Please follow this and see the extraordinary implications involved in it. Human beings are conditioned by society, by the culture in which they live, by the religion, by the economic pressures, by the climate, by the food, by the books and by the newspapers they read. They are conditioned, their whole consciousness is conditioned. And we are going to find out if there is anything beyond that conditioning. But you can find out if there is anything beyond that conditioning only when you realize that all thinking is within the pattern of consciousness. Is this clear? Now I will proceed to explain a little more.

You see, man has always sought something beyond himself, an otherness; and he called it 'God', he called it 'superconsciousness' and all kinds of names. He has started from a centre which is the totality of his consciousness. Look, sir, we will put it differently. The consciousness of man is the result of time. It is the result of the culture in which he lives, the culture being the literature, the music, the religion — and all has conditioned him. And he has built the society to which he is now a slave. Is that clear? So man is conditioned by the society which he has built, and that society further conditions him; and man is always seeking a way out of this, either consciously or unconsciously. Consciously you meditate, you read, you go to religious ceremonies and all the rest of it, trying to escape from this conditioning. Unconsciously or consciously, there is a groping, there is a seeking for something beyond the limitations of consciousness.

Thought which is the result of time is always enquiring whether it can go beyond its own conditioning, and saying that it cannot or it can, or asserting that there is something beyond. So thought which is the result of time, thought which is the whole field of consciousness — whether it is conscious or unconscious — can never discover the new. Because thought is always the old. Thought is the accumulated memory of many millennia. Thought is the result of the animal inheritance. Thought is the experience of yesterday as memory. So thought can never go beyond the limitation of consciousness.

So when you look at a tree, you are looking at the image which thought has created about that tree. When you look at your wife or husband, or at your political leader, or a religious guru and all that, you are looking at the image that thought has created about that person. Therefore you are never seeing anything new. And thought is controlled by pleasure. We function on the principle of pleasure — into which we went a little bit the other day. What we are asking now is whether it is at all possible to go beyond this limited consciousness. And to enquire into thought is a part of meditation which demands a tremendous discipline — not the discipline of control, suppression, imitation, following a method, and all the rest of that silly stuff.

Now I am going to go into this process of enquiry. The speaker is going into it; but if you want to take the journey with the speaker, you have not only to attend to what he is saying, but you have to pursue with him, not verbally, but actually.

We are going to discover whether there is a field of innocence, an innocence that has not been touched by thought at all. Whether I can look at that tree as though for the first time, whether I can look at the world with all its confusion, miseries, sorrows, deceptions, brutality, dishonesty, cruelty, war, at the whole conception of the world as though for the first time — this is an important matter. Because if I can look at it as though for the first time, my action will be totally new. Unless the mind discovers that field of innocence, whatever it does — whatever the social reforms, whatever the activity — will always be contaminated by thought because it is the product of thought, and thought is always old.

And we are asking whether consciousness, being limited, we are asking whether any movement in that consciousness is a movement of thought, conscious or unconscious. When you seek God, truth, it is still thought seeking and therefore projecting itself in terms of recognition of what it has known, and therefore what you are seeking is already known, and therefore you are not seeking at all. This is very important to understand. Therefore all seeking must totally cease — which means really, you must see actually 'what is'. That is, when you see that you are angry, jealous, competitive, greedy, selfish, brutal, violent, when you see 'what is' actually as it is, not in terms of an ideal, then you remove conflict altogether. A mind that is in conflict of any kind, at any level, becomes dull. Like two people quarrelling all the time — they are dull, stupid, they have become insensitive. Any conflict makes the mind dull. But when you see actually 'what is' without its opposite, then there is no conflict at all.

I will show you what we mean. The animal is violent. Human beings who are the result of the animal are also violent; it is part of their being to be violent, to be angry, to be jealous, to be envious, to seek power, position, prestige, and all the rest of it, to dominate, to be aggressive. Man is violent — this is shown by thousands of wars — and he has developed an ideology which he calls 'non-violence'. Please follow this closely. This country, India, has talked endlessly about it; it is one of its fanciful, ideological nonsenses. And when there is actual violence, as a war between this country and the next country, everybody is involved in it. They love it. Now, when you are actually violent and you have an ideal of non-violence, you have a conflict. You are always trying to become non-violent — which is a part of the conflict. You discipline yourself in order not to be violent — which, again, is a conflict, friction. So when you are violent and have the ideal of non-violence, you are essentially violent. To realize that you are violent is the first thing to do — not try to become non-violent. To see violence as it is, not try to translate it, not to discipline it, not to overcome it, not to suppress it, but to see it as though you are seeing it for the first time — that is to look at it without any thought.

I have explained already what we mean by looking at a tree with innocence — which is to look at it without the image. In the same way, you have to look at violence without the image which is involved in the word itself. To look at it without any movement of thought is to look at it as though you are looking at it for the first time, and therefore looking at it with innocence.

I hope you are getting this, because it is very important to understand this. If man can remove conflict within himself totally, he will create a different society altogether; and that is a radical revolution. So we are asking whether man, this conditioned entity, can break through all this conditioning so that he is no longer a Hindu, a Muslim, a communist, or a socialist with opinions or ideologies, and all that has gone. It is only possible when you begin to see things actually as they are.

You have to see the tree as the tree, not as you think the tree is. You have to look at your wife or your husband actually as she or he is, not through the image that you have built about the person. Then you are always looking at the fact, at 'what is', not trying to interpret it in terms of your personal inclination, tendency, not guided by circumstances. We are controlled by circumstances, we are guided by inclination and tendency; and, therefore, we never look at 'what actually is'. To look at 'what actually is' is innocence; the mind then has undergone a tremendous revolution.

I do not know whether you are following this. You teach a child that he is a Hindu, you teach a child that he is a dark man or a black man, and the other a Christian. You teach him, and so you control him and condition him. Now, what we are saying is that to break through this conditioning, it is necessary never to think in terms of a

Hindu, a Muslim, a communist, or a Christian, but as a human being who sees things actually as they are — which means really to die.

You know, death is, for most of us, a frightful thing. The young and the old are equally frightened of death for various reasons. Being frightened, we invent various theories — reincarnation, resurrection — and all kinds of escapes from the actual fact that there is death. Death is something unknown. As you really do not know your husband or wife but only know the image you have of the husband or the wife, so also you really do not know anything about death. You understand this? Death is something unknown, something frightening. The entity that is you has been conditioned and is full of his own anxieties, guilt, miseries, suffering, his little creative capacity, his talent to do this or that; he is all that and he is frightened to lose what he knows because his censor is the very essence of thought. If there is no thinking, there is no 'me', there is no fear at all. So thought has brought about this fear of the unknown.

There are two things involved in death. There is not only the physical ending but also the psychological ending. So man says that there is a soul that continues, that there is something permanent in me, in you, that will continue. Now, this permanent state is created by thought, whether the thought was produced by some ancient teacher, a writer, a poet, or a novelist — whom you may call a religious man, full of theories; he has created this idea of soul, of the permanent entity, by thought. And we pursue that thought and are caught by that conditioning. Like the communists — they do not believe in anything permanent; they have been taught and are thinking accordingly. In the same way as you have been taught to believe that there is something permanent, they have been taught to believe that there is nothing permanent. You are both the same, whether you believe or do not believe. You are both conditioned by belief.

Then, there is another issue involved in this, which is whether thought has a continuity. Thought continues when you give strength to it. That is, thinking everyday about yourself, about your family, about your country, about your work, about going to a job, working, working, thinking, thinking — by doing this you have created a centre which is a bundle of memories as thought. And whether that has a continuity of its own has to be enquired into. We won't go into it now because there is no time for it.

Death is something unknown. Can we come to it with innocence? You understand? Can I look at the moon shining through those leaves, and listen to those crows as though I am seeing or listening for the first time, with complete innocence of everything I have ever known? That is to die to everything I have known as yesterday. Not to carry the memory of yesterday is to die. You have to do it actually — not theorize endlessly about it. You will do it when you see the importance of it. Then you will see there is no method, there is no system, because as soon as you see something dangerous, you act immediately. In the same way, you will see that a mind that has merely a continuity of what has been can never possibly create anything new. Even in the field of science it is only when the mind is completely quiet that it discovers something totally new. So to die to yesterday, to the memories, to the hurts, to the pleasures, is to become innocent; and innocency is far more important than immortality. Innocency can never be touched by thought, but immortality is clothed with thought.

The machinery of image-making comes into being through energy, the energy whose principle is to seek pleasure. That is what we are doing. Are we not? We all want pleasure. On that principle we act. Our morality, our social relationship, our search for the so-called God, and the rest of it — all that is based on pleasure and the gratification of that pleasure. And pleasure is the continuation, by thought, of desire.

Madam, please do not take notes. This is not an examination where you take notes, go home, think about it, and then answer it afterwards. We are doing it together. You are acting and you have no time. When you are actually living, it is now, not tomorrow. If you are following this intensely, you have no time to take notes. Please listen.

Listening means learning, and learning is not accumulation. That is, when you have learned, you act from what you have learned; such learning is merely an accumulation. Again, having accumulated, according to what you have accumulated, you act; and therefore you are creating friction. If you listen, there is nothing more to do. All that you have to do is to listen. Listen as you would look at that tree, or at that moon, without any thought, without any interpretation. Just listen; there is great beauty in it. And that listening is total self-abandonment. Otherwise you cannot listen.

It is only when you are passionate you listen, and there is no passion when you cannot abandon yourself totally about anything. In the same way, if you are listening with total abandonment, you have done everything you can possibly do because then you are seeing the truth as it is, the truth of every day, of every action, of every thought, of every field. If you do not know how to see the truth of everyday movement, everyday activity, everyday work, everyday thought, you will never go beyond that, you will never find out what is beyond the limitations of consciousness.

So, as we said, the understanding of freedom brings its own discipline, and that discipline is not imitation, is not conformity. For example, you look at death very attentively; that very looking is discipline. Consciousness, as we said, is limited, and this limitation is within the reach of thought. Thought cannot break through this limitation; no amount of psychoanalysis, no amount of philosophy, no physical discipline will break through this conditioning. This can only be broken through when the whole machinery of thought is understood. Thought, as we said, is old and can never discover the new. When thought realizes that it cannot do anything, then thought itself comes to an end. Therefore there is a breaking through of the limitation of consciousness.

And this breaking through is dying to the old. This is not a theory. Don't accept it or deny it. Don't say, 'It is a very good idea'. Do it. Then you will find out for yourself that in dying to yesterday there comes innocency. Then from that innocency there is a totally different kind of action. As long as human beings have not found that, do what they will, all the reforms, all the worships, all the escapes, the worship of wealth — they have no meaning at all.

Where there is innocency which can only come about through self-abandonment, there is love. Without love and innocency there is no life; there is only torture, there is only misery, there is only conflict. And when there is innocency and love, you will know there is a totally different dimension, about which nobody can tell you. If they tell you, they are not telling the truth. Those who say they know — they do not know. But a man who has understood this comes darkly, unknowingly, on something which is of a totally different dimension — like removing the space between the observer and the observed; that state is entirely different from the state in which the observer is different from the observed.

The Collected Works of J. Krishnamurti: vol. XVII
Second Talk in Bombay, 1967

Self-knowing and Meditation

We were talking the other day, when we met here, about the necessity of a total revolution — a revolution both inward and outward. We were saying that order is essential to have peace in the world, not only order without, but primarily order within. This order is not mere routine. Order is a living thing which cannot possibly be brought about by mere intellection, by ideologies, by various forms of compulsive behaviour. We were saying, too, that thought, which has been the old, cannot function without the pattern which it has established in the past. Thought is always the old. Thought cannot possibly bring about order because order, as we said, is a living thing. And it is thought which has brought about disorder in the world.

We went into that sufficiently, I think, the other day. We said we must consider not what order is but rather what brings about disorder. Because the moment we can understand what disorder is and actually perceive it, and see, not merely intellectually, but actually the whole structure of disorder, then in the total understanding of that disorder, order will come about.

I think this is important to understand. Because most of us think that order can be brought about by repetition, that if you can go to an office for the next forty years, be an engineer or a scientist functioning in a routine, you are bringing about order. But routine is not order: routine has bred disorder. We have disorder both outwardly and inwardly. I think there is no question about this. There is general chaos, both outwardly and inwardly. Man is groping to find a way out of this chaos, asking, demanding, seeking new leaders; and if he can find a new leader, political or religious, he will follow him. That is, man is willing to follow a mechanically established routine, a purpose, a system.

But when one observes how this disorder has come into being, one sees that wherever there has been authority, especially inward authority, there must be disorder. One accepts the inward authority of another, of a teacher, of a guru, of a book, and so on. That is, by following another — his precepts, his sayings, his commands, and his authority — in a mechanical way, one hopes to bring about order within oneself. Order is necessary to have peace. But the order which we create in the pursuit of, or in following, an authority breeds disorder. You can observe what is happening in the world, especially in this country where authority still reigns, where inward authority, the demand, the urge to follow somebody is very strong and is a part of the tradition, a part of the culture. That is why there are so many ashrams, little or big, which are really concentration camps. Because there you are told exactly what to do. There is the authority of the so-called spiritual leaders. And like all concentration camps, they try to destroy you, they try to mould you into a new pattern. The communists in Russia, the regimes of dictatorship, brought about concentration camps to change opinion, to change the way of thinking, to force people. And this is exactly what is happening. The more there is chaos in the world, the more there are the so-called ashrams which are essentially concentration camps to twist the people, to mould them, to force them to a certain pattern, promising them a marvellous future. And the dullards accept this. They accept this because then they have physical security. The boss, the commissar, the guru, the authority tells them exactly what to do; and they will willingly do it because they are promised heaven or whatever it is, and in the meantime there is physical security. This type of mechanical obedience — all obedience is mechanical — does breed great disorder, as one observes from history and from the everyday incidents of life.

So, for the comprehension of disorder, one has to understand the causes of disorder. The primary cause of disorder is the pursuit or the seeking of a reality which another promises. As most of us are in confusion, as most of us are in turmoil, we would rather mechanically follow somebody who will assure us of a comfortable spiritual life. It is one of the most extraordinary things that politically we are against tyranny, dictatorship. The more liberal, the more civilized, the more free the people are, the more they abhor, they detest tyranny, politically and economically; but inwardly they would accept the authority, the tyranny of another. That is, we twist our minds, twist our thoughts and our way of life, to conform to a certain pattern established by another as the way to reality. When we do that, we are actually destroying clarity, because clarity or light has to be found by oneself, not through another, not through a book, not through any saint. Generally the saints are distorted human beings. Because they lead the so-called simple life, the others are greatly impressed; but their minds are twisted, and they create what they think is reality.

But actually to understand disorder one has to understand the whole structure of authority, not only inwardly, but also outwardly. One cannot deny outward authority. That is necessary. It is essential for any civilized society. But what we are saying is about the authority of another, including that of the speaker. There can be order only when we understand the disorder that each one of us brings about, because we are part of society; we have created the structure of society, and in that society we are caught. We, as human beings who have inherited animal instincts, have to find, as human beings, light and order. And we cannot find that light and order, or that understanding, through another — it does not matter who it is — because the experiences of another may be false. All experiences must be questioned, whether your own or of another. Experience is the continuation of a bundle of memories, which translates the response to a challenge according to its conditioning. That is, experience is, is it not, to respond to a challenge, and that experience can only respond according to its background. If you are a Hindu, or a Muslim, or a Christian, you are conditioned by your culture, by your religion, and that background projects every form of experience. And the more clever you are in interpreting that experience, the more you are respected, of course, with all that goes with it, all the circus.

So we must question, we must doubt, not only the experience of another, but also our own experience. To seek further experience through expansion of consciousness, which is being done through various forms of psychedelic drugs, is still within the field of consciousness and, therefore, very limited. So a person who is seeking experience in any form — especially the so-called religious, spiritual experience — must not only question it, doubt it, but must totally set it aside. A mind that is very clear, a mind that is full of attention and love — why should such a mind demand any more experience?

What is true cannot be invited. You can practise any amount of prayer, breathing, and all the rest of the tricks that human beings do in order to find some reality, some experience; but truth cannot be invited. That which is measurable can come, but not the immeasurable. And a man who is pursuing that which cannot be understood by a mind that is conditioned breeds disorder, not only outwardly, but inwardly.

So authority must be totally set aside, and that is one of the most difficult things to do. From childhood we are led by authority — the authority of the family, the mother and the father, the authority of the school, the teacher, and so on. There must be the authority of a scientist, the authority of a technologist. But the so-called spiritual authority is an evil thing, and that is one of the major causes of disorder because that is what has divided the world into various forms of religions, into various forms of ideologies.

So to free the mind from all authority there must be self-knowing, that is, self-knowledge. I do not mean the higher self or the Atman, which are all the inventions of the mind, the inventions of thought, inventions born out of fear. We are talking of self-knowing: knowing oneself actually as one is, not as one should be, to see that one is stupid, that one is afraid, that one is ambitious, that one is cruel, violent, greedy; the motives behind one's thought, the motives behind one's action — that is the beginning of knowing oneself. If you do not know yourself, how the structure of your mind operates, how you feel, what you think, what your motives are, why you do certain things and avoid other things, how you are pursuing pleasure — unless you know all this basically, you are capable of deceiving yourself, of creating great harm, not only to yourself, but to others. And without this basic self-knowing there can be no meditation, which I am going to talk about presently.

You know, the young people throughout the world are rejecting, revolting against the established order — an order which has made the world ugly, monstrous, chaotic. There have been wars, and for one job, there are thousands of people. Society has been built by the past generation with its ambitions, its greed, its violence, its ideologies. People, especially the young people, are rejecting all ideologies — perhaps not in this country; for we have not advanced enough, we are not civilized enough to reject all authority, all ideologies. But in rejecting ideologies they are creating their own pattern of ideology: long hair, and all the rest of it.

So mere revolt does not answer the problem. What answers the problem is to bring about order within oneself, order which is living, not a routine. Routine is deadly. You go to an office the moment you pass out of your college — if you get a job. Then, for the next forty to fifty years, you go to the office every day. You know what happens to such a mind? You have established a routine, and you repeat that routine; and you encourage your child to repeat that routine. Any man alive must revolt against it. But you will say, 'I have responsibility; placed as I am, I cannot leave it even though I would like to'. And so the world goes on, repeating the monotony, the boredom of life, its utter emptiness. Against all this, intelligence is revolting.

So there must be a new order, a new way of living. To bring about that new order, that new way of living, we must understand disorder. It is only through negation that you understand the positive, not by the pursuit of the positive. You understand, sir? When you deny, put aside, what is negative; when you understand the whole sociological and inward disorder that human beings have created; when you understand that as long as each human being is ambitious, greedy, invidious, competitive, seeking position, power, authority, he is creating disorder; and when you understand the structure of disorder — that very understanding brings about discipline, discipline not of suppression, not of imitation. Out of negation comes the right discipline, which is order.

So to understand oneself is the beginning of wisdom. Wisdom does not lie in books, nor in experience, nor in following another, nor in repeating a lot of platitudes. Wisdom comes to a mind that is understanding itself, understanding how thought is born. Have you ever questioned or asked: What is the beginning of thought, how does thought come into being? That is a very important thing to understand. Because if you can understand the beginning of thought, then perhaps you can find a mind that is not burdened with thought as a repetition of what has been. As we said, thought is always old, thought is never new. Unless you discover for yourself — not repeat what somebody says, it doesn't matter who it is — unless you find out for yourself the beginning of thought, like a seed which puts out a green leaf, you cannot possibly go beyond the limitations of yesterday.

And to find out the beginning of thought, there must be the understanding of yourself, not through analysis. Analysis takes time, like taking off the peels of an onion bit by bit. We think we can understand through analysis, through introspection, through the pursuit of a particular idea that has arisen and examining the cause of it — all that takes time. Now, when you use time as a means of understanding, then time breeds disorder. Therefore time is sorrow. You understand? If you take time to be rid, in yourself, of violence, you have established that you must be free of violence as a goal, as an ideology, and that to reach that goal, you must have time, you must cover the space between violence and that state in which there is no violence. When you have time to rid yourself of violence, you are sowing the seeds of violence all the time — which is an obvious fact. If you say to yourself, 'I will not be ambitious when I reach the top of the heap', you are in the meantime sowing the seeds of ruthlessness of an ambitious man. So the understanding of oneself is not dependent on time; it must be instantaneous. We are going into that a little bit.

We are saying the world, as it is now, is in chaos. There are wars, repetitive activity, the business of the churches — all that has bred much mischief in the world, and the continuation of all that is disorder. To bring about order, we must understand the structure of disorder. And one of the major structures of this disorder is authority. You pursue authority because of fear. You say, 'I don't know; you know, please tell me'. There is no one that can tell you. When you realize that, and when you realize that you have to find out everything entirely by yourself, inwardly, psychologically, then there is no leader, no guru, no philosopher, no saint that will help you because they are still functioning on the level of thought. Thought is always old, and thought is not a guide.

So we are going to find out the origin, the beginning of thought; and this is important. Please listen to this, not just merely to the words. You know what it is to listen? You listen, not in order to learn. Do not listen to learn, but listen with self-abandonment so that you see for yourself the true or the false. It means that you neither accept nor reject. It does not mean that you have an open mind like a sieve in which everything can be poured and nothing remains. On the contrary, because you are listening, you are highly sensitive and therefore highly critical. But your criticism will not be based on your opinion as opposed to another opinion; that is the process of thought. Please listen as you listen to those crows, without like or dislike; just listen to the sound of that boy hammering at something, without getting irritated, without losing your attention. When you listen so completely, you will find that you have nothing more to do. It is only the man who is standing on the banks of the river that speculates about the beauty of the current. When he has left the bank and is in the current, then there is no speculation, then there is no thought; there is only movement.

To understand what we are going to go into — which is the origin, the beginning of thought — one has to understand oneself; that is, one has to learn about oneself. Acquiring knowledge about oneself and learning about oneself are two different things. You can accumulate knowledge about yourself by watching yourself, by examining yourself. And from what you have learned, from the accumulation you begin to act; and therefore in that action you are further acquiring. You understand? What you have learned, what you have accumulated is already in the past. All accumulation is in the past, and from the past you begin to observe and accumulate more. Whereas learning is not accumulation. Learning is — as you watch, you are moving with the action itself; therefore there is no residue in your learning, but always learning. Learning is an active-present of the word, not the past-present. We are going to learn, but not from what has been accumulated. In learning a language, you have to accumulate. You have to know the words, you have to learn the various verbs, and so on; and after having learned, you begin to use them. Here it is not at all like that. Seeing a danger brings about an immediate action. When you see a danger like a precipice, there is an immediate action.

So what we are going to do is to find out, to understand the beginning, the origin of thinking. And to do that, you have to listen and go with it, which means you must give attention. Attention is possible only when you are deeply enquiring — which means, you are actually free to enquire, and you are not bound by what some people have said and so on.

Now, all life is energy, it is an endless movement. And that energy in its movement creates a pattern which is based on self-protection and security — that is, survival. Energy, movement, getting caught in a pattern of survival, and the repeating of that pattern — this is the beginning of thought. Thought is mind. Energy is movement, that movement caught in the pattern of survival, and the repetition of survival in the sense of pleasure, of fear — that is the beginning of thought.

Thought is the response of accumulated memory, accumulated patterns — which is what you are doing as a Hindu, a Muslim, a Parsi, a Christian, a communist, a socialist and so on. We function in patterns, and the repetition of that pattern is the repetition of thought, repeating over and over again. That is what you are doing as a Hindu, a Muslim or a Parsi — the pattern established by repetition as survival, in the framework of a culture which is Hindu, Muslim or Parsi. This is actually what is going on within each one. Thought has always established a pattern, and if the old pattern is not suitable, it establishes another pattern. If capitalism is not right, then communism is right; that is a new pattern. Or if Hinduism or Christianity is not convenient, you form another pattern.

So the repetition of that pattern conditions the brain cells themselves, which are matter. Thought is matter. One can discover this for oneself. You must discover it, not because the speaker is telling you — that has no value whatsoever. It is like a man who is hungry being told how marvellous the food is, and being fed on theories. That is what is happening in this country; you are fed on theories and ideologies — the Buddhist ideology, the Hindu ideology, the Shankaracharya ideology, and all the rest of it. Therefore your minds are empty. You are fed on words; that is why there is disorder. That is why all this must be thrown away, so that we start anew. To start anew one must understand this whole structure of thought. Now, you understand this structure of thought only when you begin to understand yourself as a living movement — not 'having understood, you add more to it'; then it becomes a dead thing. You are a living thing within the framework of a culture; and that culture, that tradition, that authority holds you. And within that framework of consciousness is disorder. To understand this whole process and to go very much further — which we are going to do now — is meditation.

Meditation is not the repetitive formula of mantras, of breathing regularly, of sitting in a certain posture, practising awareness, practising attention — these are all utterly mechanical. We are talking of a living thing. And you have practised these mechanical things for centuries upon centuries. Those who have practised them are dead, and their visions are projections from their own past, from their own conditioning. But we are talking of a living meditation, not a mechanical, repetitive, disciplinary meditation. Unless you know what meditation is — like unless you know what death is — there is no new culture, nothing new is born.

You know, culture is one of the most marvellous things, not the dead culture about which you talk endlessly — the Indian culture, the Hindu culture; that is buried, gone, finished. The living culture is what is actually taking place now. To see the confusion, the mess, the terrible misery, and out of that to grow and to flower — that is culture, not going back to your dead parents.

So we are going to find out together and take a journey together into this question of what is meditation. You can only ask that question when you have gone through knowing yourself. You cannot ask, 'What is meditation?' unless you know yourself, unless you have an understanding of yourself, unless you have looked at yourself as much as possible. As I said, 'looking at yourself' is instantaneous; the totality of yourself is revealed in the instant, not in time. You can actually see with your eyes a tree, a flower, a human being next to you. You cannot see the totality of that tree or the totality of the human being next to you if you have an image about that tree or about that person. This is obvious. It is only when the image is not, that you can see completely. The image is the observer, is the centre from which you observe. When there is a centre from which you observe, there is a space between the observer and the observed. You do not have to pay such enormous attention to what is being said, you can observe this yourself. As long as there is an image about your wife, about your husband, about a tree, about anything, it is the image which is the centre which is looking. So there is separation between the observer and the observed. This is important to understand. We are going into it presently.

First of all, let us remove erroneous ideas about concentration. It is one of the favourite sayings of the meditator or the teacher who practises or teaches meditation that people must learn concentration — that is, to concentrate on one thought, drive out every other thought and fix your mind on that one thought only. This is a most stupid thing to do. Because when you do that, you are merely resisting, you are having a battle between the demand that you must concentrate on one thing, and your mind wandering to all kinds of other things. Whereas you have to be attentive not only to the one thought but also to where the mind is wandering, totally attentive to every movement of the mind. This is possible only when you don't deny any movement, when you don't say, 'My mind wanders away, my mind is distracted'. There is no such thing as distraction. Because, when the mind wanders off, it indicates that it is interested in something else.

So one has to understand the whole question of control. But, unfortunately, we cannot go into this this evening as there is no time. We human beings are such controlled, dead entities. This does not mean that we must explode in doing what we want to do — which we do anyhow secretly. But there comes a discipline with love. So I will go into it very quickly.

Meditation is not control of thought. Meditation, when thought is controlled, only breeds conflict in the mind. But when you understand the structure of thought and the origin of thought, then thought will not interfere, as I have explained to you just now. Therefore you will see that thought has its place — which is, you must go to the office, you must go to your house, speak a language; there thought must function. But when you have understood the whole structure of thinking, that very understanding of the structure of thinking is its own discipline, which is not imitation, which has nothing to do with suppression.

The cells of the brain have been conditioned to survive within a given pattern, as a Hindu, a Muslim, a Parsi, a Christian, a Catholic or a communist. As the brain has been conditioned to survive for centuries upon centuries, it has the pattern of repetition; so the brain itself becomes the major factor of restless enquiry. You will see it for yourself when you go into it.

So the problem is to bring about absolute quietness in the brain cells themselves, which means no seeking of self-importance and of self-continuance. You understand? We must survive at the physical level, and we must die at the psychological level. It is only where there is death, at the psychological level, of a thousand yesterdays that the brain cells are quiet. And this does not come about through any form of manipulation of thought, repetition of mantras — all that is immature. But it comes about only when you understand the whole movement of thought, which is yourself. So the brain cells become extraordinarily quiet, without any movement, except to respond to the outward reactions.

So the brain itself being quiet, the totality of the mind is completely silent, and that silence is a living thing. It is not the product of any guru, of any book, of any ashram, of any leader, of any authority, or of any drug. You can take a drug, a chemical, to make your mind quiet, or you can mesmerize yourself to be quiet. But that is not the living stillness of a mind that has gone into itself deeply, and therefore is tremendously attentive and highly sensitive. It is only such a mind that can understand what love is. Love is not desire or pleasure. All that we have is desire and pleasure, which we call love. 'I love my wife, I love my God', and so on — all that is based on fear, pleasure, and sensation.

So a man who has understood and really gone into this will bring about order, first, within himself. If there is order in oneself, there is order in the world. If each one of you will really bring about order in yourself, you will have a living order, a new society, a new life. But to do that, you have to destroy the old patterns of life. The old patterns of life cannot be broken except through understanding yourself, and out of that understanding comes love.

You know, man has talked about love endlessly: love your neighbour, love God, be kind. But, now, you are neither kind nor generous. You are so concentrated on yourself that you have no love. And without love there is only sorrow. This is not a mere aphorism for you to repeat. You have to find that, you have to come upon it. You have to work hard for it. You have to work with the understanding of yourself, ceaselessly, with a passion. Passion is not lust; a man who does not know what passion is will never know love. Love can come into being only when there is total self-abandonment. And it is only love that can bring about order, a new culture, a new way of life.

The Collected Works of J. Krishnamurti: vol. XVII
Third Talk in Bombay 1967

The Ending of Sorrow

This is the last talk. I think, during the last three meetings that we have had here, we have more or less indicated in what direction one has to make one's way. Because the world, as we see now, is becoming more and more chaotic, more and more violent, almost anarchical, antisocial. There is war, there is such exploitation, ruthless efficiency, mismanagement, bad government, and so on. We can enumerate the many problems that we — each one of us — have to face: a world that we have created out of our greed, out of our sorrow, conflict, and the desire for pleasure, the urge to dominate, to seek a position.

We could go on enumerating all the many problems in more detail. But description and explanation have very little value when we are confronted with the problem. And unfortunately we are so easily satisfied with explanations. We think words will actually solve our problems, and so there is a Niagara of words, not only at this meeting, but also right throughout the world. Everybody talks endlessly and there are innumerable theories, new ideologies and, unfortunately, new leaders — both political and religious — and there is every form of propaganda to convince another of what he should do, of what he should think. And it is one of the most difficult things to find out how to think. Our problem is not only social, economic, and so on, but much more a religious problem, a problem of crisis in the whole of consciousness. And, there, it almost becomes meaningless if one depends on words, explanations, or definitions. Perhaps these talks may have pointed out not what to think but how to think. We are slaves of propaganda. We have been told what to think — the Gita, the Koran, the Bible, the priest, Marx-Lenin theories, the innumerable ideologies. But we do not know, I am afraid, how to think very deeply and to see the limitation of thought.

One of our major problems, probably the only problem, is sorrow. Man has tried through every form to resolve, to end sorrow; he has tried to escape from it, he has worshipped it, he has given many explanations. But man, endlessly, from the moment he is born until he dies, lives in this sorrow, in this grief. It seems to me that unless one resolves that issue not verbally, not by ideas or by explanations, but actually by stepping out of the stream of this incessant sorrow, one's problems will multiply. You may be very rich, you may have power, position, prestige, status, and you may be very clever, you may have all the brains in the world, with great information, but, I am afraid, all those things are not going to resolve the human demands, the human urgency of resolving one of the most fundamental questions, which is sorrow. Because with the ending of sorrow is the beginning of wisdom. Wisdom — not cunningness, not knowledge, not ideologies — comes only with the ending of sorrow; and without wisdom we cannot solve our human problem, not only outwardly, but also inwardly.

Man, as one observes historically and also from one's own life or one's own everyday activity, is caught in the principle of pleasure and sorrow. We are guided by pleasure. Most of us want pleasure only, and we are pursuing it most subtly. When we seek truth — as people say they do when they are religious — we are still seeking this principle of pleasure. Where there is pleasure in any form, there must also be sorrow: one cannot be pursued without the other. There is not only sensuous pleasure, sensuous enjoyment, but also — if one is a little more refined, a little more cultured, a little more intellectual — the pleasure of reformation, of doing good, of altering society. Writing books, entering into politics, and other endless activities of the fulfilment of desire — all that is the continuation of pleasure. If one observes one's own life, if one is at all aware, even casually, one will find that we are guided by our inclination, by our tendency. Inclination and tendency are the outcome of this constant demand for greater and greater satisfaction of pleasure. After all, all virtue is based on this principle of pleasure. Without understanding this pleasure, there is no ending of sorrow. I would like to go into it rather deeply.

Is all life a pleasure? Is all life a conflict and misery, an endless series of battles, outside and inside? A life which is made into a battlefield — that is all we know. We may spin theories, we may endlessly talk about theological concepts, social improvements, and criticism of what shall be. But unless we understand this extraordinary demand for pleasure, it seems to me, we shall be caught in the current of endless conflict and sorrow. To understand pleasure is not to deny it, because pleasure is one of the basic demands of life, like enjoyment. When you see a beautiful tree, a lovely sunset, a nice smile on a face, light on a leaf, then you really enjoy it, there is a great delight.

Beauty is something that is not pleasure. The sense of beauty is not in a building, in a picture, in a poem, in holding the hand of another, in looking at a mountain or a river — these are still sensations, however pleasurable. Beauty is something entirely different. To understand actually what beauty is — not intellectually, not verbally — one must understand pleasure.

You know, man has been denied pleasure through religion, through worship of an idea, through the saints and the missionaries, by the sannyasis and the monks throughout the world. They have consistently denied pleasure to man. They say it is wrong, it is something evil, something to be put away. They say that a mind that is full of pleasure, or is seeking pleasure, can never find reality, God, and that therefore you should torture yourself. But such persons come to God with a twisted, tortured, petty, little mind. A mind that has been squeezed by society, by culture, is no longer a mind free, alive, vibrant, capable, unafraid. And most human minds are tortured. They may not know it, they may not be aware of it. They may be so completely occupied with their families, with earning a livelihood, with achieving a position, that they may not be aware of the total content of their being.

Man is always seeking: seeking a purpose, seeking a goal, seeking satisfaction; and the satisfaction in the highest he calls God. So we are always seeking, seeking, seeking. We are always feeling that something is missing, and so we try to fill that void in ourselves, that loneliness, that emptiness, that weary, exhausting, meaningless existence of life with lots of ideas, with significance, with purposes, ultimately seeking satisfaction in a permanency which will never be disturbed. And that state of permanency we call by a thousand names — God, samadhi, and so on; one can invent names. We are endlessly seeking, and we never ask why we are seeking. The obvious answer is that we are dissatisfied, unhappy, unfortunate, lonely, unloved, fearful. We need something to cling to, we need somebody to protect us — the father, the mother, and so on — and so we are seeking. When we are seeking, we are always finding. Unfortunately, we will always find when we are seeking.

So the first thing is not to seek. You understand? You all have been told that you must seek, experiment with truth, find out truth, go after it, pursue it, chase it, and that you must discipline, control yourself. And then somebody comes along and says, 'Don't do all that. Don't seek at all'. Naturally, your reaction is either to ask him to go away or you turn your back, or you find out for yourself why he says such a thing — not accept, not deny, but question. And what are you seeking?

Enquire about yourself. You are seeking; you are saying that you are missing something in this life inwardly — not at the level of technique or having a petty job or more money. What is it that we are seeking? We are seeking because in us there is such deep dissatisfaction with our family, with society, with culture, with our own selves, and we want to satisfy, to go beyond this gnawing discontent that is destroying. And why are we discontented? I know discontent can very easily be satisfied. Give a young man who has been discontented — a communist or a revolutionary — a good job, and he forgets all about it. Give him a nice house, a nice car, a nice garden, a good position, and you will see that discontent disappears. If he can achieve an ideological success, that discontent disappears too. But you never ask why you are discontented — not the people who have jobs, and who want better jobs. We must understand the root cause of discontent before we can examine the whole structure and the meaning of pleasure and, therefore, of sorrow.

You know, sirs, from school days until one dies, we are educated, we are conditioned in comparison. I compare myself with somebody else. Do watch yourself; please listen to what I am saying, and see how your mind works. You have a double task: you have not only to listen to the speaker but also, in listening to him, to observe your own state of mind actually. So you need a certain attention, a certain awareness of both the speaker and what he is saying, and observing yourself. But if you are listening — actually listening in the sense of not trying to understand, not trying to translate what the speaker is speaking, not condemning, not adjusting, not denying or accepting — you will see that there is neither the speaker nor yourself, but there is only the fact, there is only 'what is'. That is the art of listening: not listening to the speaker or to your own opinions and judgements, but to 'what actually is'. We are always comparing ourselves with somebody else. If I am dull, I want to be more clever. If I am shallow, I want to be deep. If I am ignorant, I want to be more clever, more knowledgeable. I am always comparing myself, measuring myself against others — a better car, better food, a better home, a better way of thinking. Comparison breeds conflict. And do you understand through comparison? When you compare two pictures, two pieces of music, two sunsets, when you compare that tree with another tree, do you understand either? Or do you understand something only when there is no comparison at all?

So is it possible to live without comparison of any kind, never translating yourself in terms of comparison with another or with some idea or with some hero or with some example? Because when you are comparing, when you are measuring yourself with 'what should be' or 'what has been', you are not seeing 'what is'. Please listen to this. It is very simple, and therefore probably you, being clever, cunning, will miss it. We are asking whether it is possible to live in this world without any comparison at all. Don't say no. You have never done it. You won't say, 'I cannot do it; it is impossible because all my conditioning is to compare'. In a schoolroom a boy is compared with another, and the teacher says, 'You are not as clever as the other'. The teacher destroys B when he is comparing B with A. That process goes on through life.

We think that comparison is essential for progress, for understanding, for intellectual development. I don't think it is. When you are comparing one picture with the other, you are not looking at either of them. You can only look at one picture when there is no comparison. So, in the same way, is it possible to live a life never comparing, psychologically, yourself with another? Never comparing with Rama, Sita, Gita, whoever it is, with the hero, with your gods, with your ideals. A mind that is not comparing at all, at any level, becomes extraordinarily efficient, becomes extraordinarily alive, because then it is looking at 'what is'.

Look, sir, I am shallow; I compare myself with another who is supposed to be very deep, capable, and profound in his thinking and in his way of living. I, being shallow, narrow, limited, compare myself with that person, and I struggle to be like him. I imitate, quote, follow, and try to destroy myself in order to be like him; and this conflict goes on endlessly. Whereas if there is no comparison at all, how do I know I am dull? Because you tell me? Because I cannot get a job? Because I am no good at school? How do I know I am dull if there is no comparison at all? Therefore I am what I am; I am in that state from which I can move, I can discover, I can change. But when I am comparing myself with another, the change will invariably be superficial. Please do listen to all this, it is your life. Whereas if there is no comparison, 'what is' is; from there I move. This is one of the fundamental principles of life, that modern life has conditioned man to compare, to compete, to struggle endlessly, caught in a battle with another. I can only look at 'what is' when there is no comparison. So I understand, not verbally, but actually, that comparison is a most childish, immature thing.

Sir, where there is love, is there a comparison? When you love somebody with your heart, with your mind, with your body, with your entire being — not be possessive, not be dominating, not say, 'It is mine' — is there any comparison? Only when there is no comparison, can you look at 'what is'. If we understand that, then we can proceed to find out, to enquire into the whole structure of pleasure.

Not to compare 'what is', not only with the future, but also with what has been the past — this demands tremendous attention. You understand? I had a pleasure yesterday — sensuous pleasure, an idea which has brought an extraordinary light, a cloud which I saw full of light yesterday, but which now I don't see at all — and I want that back. So I compare the present with what has been and I am going to compare the present with what should be. It requires extraordinary intelligence and sensitivity to be free of this comparative evaluation. One must have intelligence and sensitivity completely; then only can one understand 'what is'. Then you see you are passionate, and then you have the energy to pursue 'what is'. But you lose that energy when you are comparing 'what is' with 'what has been' or 'what should be'.

Now, I hope that is clear — not intellectually because that has no meaning at all; you may just as well get up and go away. But if you really understand this, then you can look at pleasure; you do not compare it with the pleasure that you have had yesterday, or with the pleasure that you are going to have tomorrow, but you look at the actual mind that is seeking pleasure. Man has to understand this principle of pleasure, not just say, 'I want pleasure'. If you want pleasure, you must also have pain and also sorrow with it; you cannot have one without the other. And if you pursue pleasure in any form, you are creating a world of conflict. When you say, 'I am a Hindu' — you know all the rest of the labels one gives to oneself — then you become very important. Like when you worship one river, you deny all other rivers; when one family becomes all-important, you deny all the other families, and that is why families are a danger; when you worship one tree, one god, then you deny all trees, all gods. And that is what is happening: when you worship your own particular little nation, then you deny all other nations; then you are ready to fight, to go to battle and kill each other.

So pleasure is embedded in the worship of gods, searching for truth, saying, 'my nation', 'my family', 'my position'; in all this, pleasure is involved, and this pleasure is creating untold mischief. We have to understand this, not deny it, because the moment you deny, it is like cutting your arm off or blinding yourself so that you will not have the pleasure of seeing a beautiful cloud, a beautiful woman, or a lovely tree. So we have to understand the extraordinary importance of pleasure and how it comes into being. And when you understand it, you see what significance pleasure has, as we are going to see now.

You know, you have been told by the religious people of the world that you must be without desire. It is one of the edicts of the so-called religious people that you must strive to be without desire, to be desireless. That is sheer nonsense because when you see anything, you have already desire. Desire is a reaction. When you see a brilliant colour, look at it. You know, one of the most beautiful things is colour; colour is God. Look at it, do not say, 'I like red', or 'I like blue'; but just watch the colour of a cloud, the colour of a sari, the colour of a leaf that has just come in the spring. When you do look, you will find that there is no pleasure at all, but sheer beauty. Beauty, like love, is not desire, is not pleasure.

And it is important to understand this whole question of desire, which is quite simple. I do not know why people make such a lot of ado about it. You can see how it comes into being. There is perception; then sensation, contact, and desire. Do you follow? I see a beautiful car — first, perception. Then the sensation of it, then you touch it, and there is the desire to own it — desire. First seeing, perception; then observation, sensation, contact, desire. It is as simple as that. Now the problem begins. Then thought comes in and thinks about that desire, which becomes pleasure. That is, sir, I see a beautiful mountain with deep valleys, covered with snow, bright in the morning light, full of aloofness and splendour. I see it. Then thought begins to say, 'How beautiful! I wish I could always be seeing it!' Thought — which is memory responding to what it sees — says, 'I wish I could live there!' Or I see a beautiful face; I think about that face; then thinking constantly about it creates the pleasure. Sex — the pleasure that you had, and you think about it, the image — the more you think about it, the more the pleasure; so then desire. Thought brings about the continuity of pleasure. It is very simple when you look into it.

Then one asks, 'Is it possible for thought not to touch desire?' You follow it? That is your problem. When you see something extraordinarily beautiful, full of life and beauty, you must never let thought come in, because the moment thought touches it, thought being old, it will pervert it into pleasure and, therefore, there arises the demand for pleasure and for more and more of pleasure; and when it is not given, there is conflict, there is fear. So is it possible to look at a thing without thought? To look you must be tremendously alive, not paralysed. But the religious people have said to you, 'Be paralysed, come to reality crippled'. But you can never come to reality crippled. To see reality, you must have a clear mind, unperverted, innocent, unconfused, untortured, free; then only can you see reality. If you see a tree, you must look at it with clear eyes, without the image. When thought thinks about desire — and thought will always think about desire — out of that, it derives pleasure. There is the image which thought has created about the object, and constant thinking about that image, that symbol, that picture, gives rise to pleasure. You see a beautiful head, you look at it. Thought says, 'It is a beautiful head, it's a nice head, it has got nice hair'. It begins to think about it, and it is pleasurable.

To see something without thought does not mean that you should stop thinking — that is not the point. But you must be aware when thought interferes with desire, knowing that desire is perception, sensation, contact. You must be aware of the whole mechanism of desire, and also when thought precipitates instantly on it. And that requires not only intelligence but awareness, so that you are aware when you see something extraordinarily beautiful or extraordinarily ugly. Then the mind is not comparing: beauty is not ugliness, and ugliness is not beauty. So with the understanding of pleasure you can investigate sorrow.

Without knowing sorrow, do what you will — climb the highest social ladder or the bureaucratic ladder or the religious ladder or the political ladder — you will always be creating mischief, either in the name of God or in the name of your country or your party or your society or your ideology; you will be a mischief monger. This is obvious.

So what is sorrow? Again, please look at 'what is', not at 'what should be'. Because now if you have gone into it, you are not comparing any more, but you are actually looking at 'what is'. Therefore you have got energy to look, and that energy is not being dissipated in comparing. One of the problems of man is how to have energy. Again, the religious people with their petty, little minds have said, 'To have energy, you must be a bachelor; to have energy you must starve, fast, eat one meal, wear a loincloth, get up at two in the morning and pray' — it is all idiotic because you are thereby destroying yourself, you are destroying energy. Energy comes when you look at actually 'what is', which means no dissipation of energy in comparison.

We are saying, 'What is sorrow?' Man has tried to overcome sorrow in so many ways — through worship, through escape, through drink, through entertainment — but it is always there. Sorrow has to be understood as you would understand any other thing. Do not deny it, do not suppress it, do not try to overcome it; but understand it, look at what it is. What is sorrow? Do you know what sorrow is? Must I tell you? Sorrow is when you lose somebody whom you think you love; sorrow is when you cannot fulfil totally, completely; sorrow is when you are denied opportunity, capacity; sorrow is when you want to fulfil and there is no way to fulfil; sorrow is when you are confronted by your own utter emptiness, loneliness; and sorrow is burdened with self-pity. Do you know what 'self-pity' is? Self-pity is when you complain about yourself unconsciously or consciously, when you are pitying yourself, when you say, 'I cannot do anything against the environment in which I am, placed as I am'; when you call yourself a pest, bemoaning your own lot. And so there is sorrow.

To understand sorrow, first, one has to be aware of this self-pity. It is one of the factors of sorrow. When someone dies, you are left and you become aware of how lonely you are. Or if someone dies, you are left without any money, you are insecure. You have lived on others and you begin to complain, you begin to have self-pity. So one of the causes of sorrow is self-pity. That is a fact, like the fact that you are lonely; that is 'what is'. Look at self-pity, do not try to overcome it, do not deny it or say, 'What am I to do with it?' The fact is: there is self-pity. The fact is: you are lonely. Can you look at it without any comparison of how extraordinarily secure you were yesterday, when you had that money or that person or that capacity — whatever it is? Just look at it; then you will see that self-pity has no place at all. That does not mean that you accept the condition as it is.

One of the factors of sorrow is the extraordinary loneliness of man. You may have companions, you may have gods, you may have a great deal of knowledge, you may be extraordinarily active socially, talking endless gossip about politics — and most politicians gossip anyhow — and still this loneliness remains. Therefore man seeks to find significance in life and invents a significance, a meaning. But the loneliness still remains. So can you look at it without any comparison, just see it as it is, without trying to run away from it, without trying to cover it up, or to escape from it? Then you will see that loneliness becomes something entirely different.

Man must be alone. We are not alone. We are the result of a thousand influences, a thousand conditionings, psychological inheritances, propaganda, culture. We are not alone, and therefore we are second-hand human beings. When one is alone, totally alone, neither belonging to any family, though one may have a family, nor belonging to any nation, to any culture, to any particular commitment, there is the sense of being an outsider — outsider to every form of thought, action, family, nation. And it is only the one who is completely alone who is innocent. It is this innocency that frees the mind from sorrow.

And a mind ridden with sorrow will never know what love is. Do you know what love is? There is no love when there is space between the observer and the observed.

You know what space is? The space between you and that tree, between you and what you think you should be. There is space when there is the centre or the observer. You understand this? Again, this is very simple, and this becomes extraordinarily complex much later. But first begin with it simply. There is this microphone in front of the speaker. That microphone is in space. But the microphone also creates the space. There is a house with four walls. There is not only space outside but there is also space within the four walls. And there is space between you and the tree, between you and your neighbour, and between you and your wife. As long as there is this space between you and your neighbour, your wife, your husband, or anybody, this space implies that there is a centre which creates the space. Are you following this? When you look at the stars, there is you who are looking at the stars and the marvellous sky of an evening with brilliant stars, clear, cool air — you, the observer, and the observed.

So you are the centre who is creating the space. When you look at that tree, you have an image about yourself and about the tree; that image is the centre which is looking, and therefore there is space. And as we said, love is when there is no space — that is, when there is no space which the observer creates between himself and the tree. You have an image about your wife, and your wife has an image about you. You have built up that image for ten years or for two years or for a day, through her pleasure, your pleasure, through her insults, your insults; you have built it up through nagging, dominating, and all the rest of it. And the contact between these two images is called 'relationship'. It is only when there is no image that there is love — which means there is no space, not sensuous space, not physical space; but, inwardly, there is no space, just as there is beauty when there is no space.

There is space when there is no self-abandonment. You know, we are talking about something you do not understand. You have never done it. You have never removed the space between yourself and your wife, between yourself and the tree, or between yourself and the stars and the sky or the clouds; you have never actually looked. You don't know what beauty is because you don't know what love is. You talk about it, you write about it, but you have never felt it because you have never known, except probably at rare intervals, this total self-abandonment. Because it is that centre that creates the space round itself. And as long as there is that space, there is neither love nor beauty. That is why our lives are so empty, so callous.

You go to an office — I don't know why. You say, 'I have to go because I have responsibility, I have to earn, I have to support my family'. I don't know why you must do anything. You are slaves, that is all. You have never observed when you are looking at a tree or looking at the face of a person opposite to you. When you do look at that face, you are looking from a centre. The centre creates the space between yourself and that person. And to overcome that space, people are taking drugs like LSD. When you take that drug, it makes your mind extraordinarily sensitive; a chemical change takes place, and then you see that space disappears completely. Not that I have taken it. (Laughter) Those are artificial means and, therefore, not real. Those are all instant happiness, instant paradise, instant bliss. You can't get it that way.

So without love and beauty, there is no truth. Your saints, your gods, your priests, your books have denied this. That is why you are in such a sorrowful plight. You would rather talk about the Gita, the Koran, the Bible, than love. This means you look at the dirty roads, the squalor, the filth along these roads, and you put up with it. You co-operate with dirt, and you do not know when not to co-operate. You co-operate with the system, and you do not know when to say, 'No, I won't co-operate, and it does not matter what happens'. But when you say so, it is because you love, because you have beauty, not because you revolt. Then you will know, when you have this, there is beauty, love, and there is the perception of 'what is' which is love. Then the mind can go immeasurably beyond itself.

But you have to work, you have to work like fury every day, as you go to your office every day. You have to work hard, not to achieve love, because you cannot achieve love anymore than you can achieve humility — it is only the vain man that talks and achieves humility, but he is always vain. Like humility, you cannot cultivate love, not cultivate beauty; without being aware you cannot see what is truth. But if you are aware — not awareness of some mysterious nature — if you are just aware of what you are doing, of what you are thinking, how you look, how you walk, how you eat, what you talk about, then out of that awareness you will begin to see the nature of pleasure, desire, and sorrow, and the utter loneliness and boredom of man. And then you will begin to come upon that thing called the 'space'. And where there is space between yourself and the object, then you know there is no love.

Without love, do what you will — reform, bring about a new social order, talk about endless ideological improvement — all that creates agony. So it is up to you. There is no leader, there is no guru. There is nobody to tell you what to do. You have to be a light unto yourself. Therefore you are alone, alone amidst the mad, brutal world. That is why one has to be an oasis in a desert of ideas. And the oasis comes into being when there is love.

The Collected Works of J. Krishnamurti: vol. XVII
Fourth Talk in Bombay 1967

II

Questions and Answers

Questions and Answers

Question: I read in the newspaper today your statement that to solve man's problems, what is needed is not an economic or social revolution but a religious revolution. What do you mean by religious revolution?

KRISHNAMURTI: First of all, let us find out what we mean by religion. What is religion for most of us — not the theory of what religion should be, but the actual fact? For most of us, religion is obviously a series of dogmas, traditions, what the Upanishads or the Gita or the Bible has said; or it is made up of the experiences, visions, hopes, ideas which have sprung from our conditioned minds, from our minds which have been shaped according to the Hindu, the Christian, or the communist pattern. We start with a particular conditioning and have experiences based on it. What we call religion is prayer, ritual, dogma, wishing to find God, the acceptance of authority, and a vast number of superstitions, is it not? But is that religion? A man who is really trying to find out what is true must surely abandon all that, must he not? He must totally discard the authority of the guru, of the Upanishads, and the authority of his own experiences so that, being purged of all authority, his mind is capable of discovery. That means you must cease to be a Hindu, a Christian, a Buddhist; you must see the absurdity of that whole business and break away from it. And will you? Because if you do, you are against the present society and may lose your job. So fear dominates the mind, and you go on accepting authority.

What we call religion, then, is not religion at all. Whether we believe in God or do not believe in God depends upon our conditioning. You believe in God, and the communist believes in no-God. What is the difference? There is no difference whatsoever because you are trained to believe, and he is trained not to believe. Therefore a man who is seriously enquiring must totally reject that process, must he not? — reject it because he understands the whole significance of it.

Being insecure, frightened, inwardly insufficient, we identify ourselves with a country, with an ideology, or with a belief in God, and we can see what is happening throughout the world. Every religion, though they all profess love, brotherhood, and all the rest of it, is actually separating man from man. You are a Sikh and I am a Hindu, he is a Muslim and somebody else is a Buddhist. Seeing all this confusion and separation, one realizes there must be a different kind of thinking, but the different kind of thinking obviously cannot come into being as long as one remains a Hindu, a Christian, or what you will. To be free of all that, you have to know yourself, the whole structure of your being; you have to see why you accept, why you follow authority, which is fairly obvious. You want success; you want to be assured that there is a God on whom you can rely in moments of trouble. A man who is really joyous, happy, never thinks about God. We think about God when we are in misery, conflict, but we have created the misery, the conflict, and without understanding the whole process of it, merely to enquire after God leads to utter illusion.

So the religious revolution of which I am talking is not the revival or reformation of any particular religion but the total freedom from all religions and ideologies — which means, really, freedom from the society which has created them. Surely, a man who is ambitious cannot be a religious man. A man who is ambitious does not know love, though he may talk about it. A man may not be ambitious in the worldly sense, but if he wants to be a saint, a spiritual somebody, if he wants to achieve a result in the next world, he is still ambitious. So the mind must not only be stripped of all ceremonies, beliefs, and dogmas, but it must also be free of envy. The total freedom of man is the religious revolution, for only then will he be able to approach life entirely differently and cease to create problem after problem.

You have probably listened to all this only verbally or intellectually because you say to yourself, 'What would I do in life if I had no ambition? I should be destroyed by society'. I wonder if you would be destroyed by society. The moment you understand society and reject the whole structure on which it is based — ambition, envy, the pursuit of success, the religious dogmas, beliefs and superstitions — you are outside of society and can therefore think of the whole problem anew, and perhaps then there will be no problem. But you have probably listened only on the verbal level and will continue with the same old thing tomorrow; you will read the Gita or the Bible, go to your guru or a priest, and all the rest of it. You may listen to all this and accept it intellectually, verbally, but your life continues in the opposite direction, so you have merely created another conflict; therefore it is much better not to listen at all because you have enough conflicts, enough problems, without introducing a new one. It is very nice to sit and listen to what is being said here, but if it has no relationship to your actual life, it is much better to shut your ears, because if you hear the truth and do not live it, your life becomes a hideous confusion, the sorrowful mess which it is.

The Collected Works of J. Krishnamurti: vol. X
New Delhi, October 10, 1956

Question: We find ourselves living in fear of war, of losing a job, if we have one, in fear of terrorism, of the violence of our children, of being at the very mercy of inept politicians. How do we meet life as it is today?

KRISHNAMURTI: How do you meet it? One must take it for granted that the world is becoming more and more violent — it is obvious. The threats of war are also very obvious, and also the very strange phenomenon that our children are becoming violent. One remembers a mother coming to see us in India some time ago. In the Indian tradition mothers are held in very great respect, and this mother was horrified because, she said, her children had beaten her — an unheard-of thing in India. So this violence is spreading all over the world. And there is this fear of losing a job, as the questioner says. Facing all this, knowing all this, how does one meet life as it is today?

I don't know. I know how to meet it for myself, but one doesn't know how you will meet it. First, what is life, what is this thing called existence, full of sorrow, over-population, inept politicians, all the trickery, dishonesty, bribery that is going on in the world? How does one meet it? Surely, one must first enquire what does it mean to live? What does it mean to live in this world as it is? How do we live our daily life, actually, not theoretically, not philosophically or idealistically, but actually how do we live our daily life? If we examine it or are aware of it seriously, it is a constant battle, constant struggle, effort after effort. Having to get up in the morning is an effort. What shall we do? We cannot possibly escape from it. One used to know several people who said that the world was impossible to live in, and they withdrew totally to some Himalayan mountains and disappeared. That is merely an avoidance, an escape from reality, as it is to lose oneself in a commune, or join some guru with vast estates and get lost in that. Obviously, those people do not solve the problems of daily life nor enquire into the change, the psychological revolution of a society. They escape from all this. And we, if we do not escape and are actually living in this world as it is, what shall we do? Can we change our life? To have no conflict at all in our life, because conflict is part of violence — is that possible? This constant struggle to be something is the basis of our life, to struggle, to struggle.

Can we, as human beings, living in this world, change ourselves? That is really the question — radically, psychologically transform ourselves, not eventually, not admitting time. For a serious man, a really religious man, there is no tomorrow. This is rather a hard saying, that there is no tomorrow; there is only the rich worship of today. Can we live this life wholly, and actually, daily, transform our relationship with each other? That is the real issue, not what the world is, for the world is us. Please see this: the world is you and you are the world. This is an obvious, terrible fact, a challenge that must be met completely — that is, to realize that we are the world with all its ugliness, that we have contributed to all this, that we are responsible for all this, all that is happening in the Middle East, in Africa and all the craziness that is going on in this world, we are responsible for it. We may not be responsible for the deeds of our grandfathers and great-grandfathers — slavery, thousands of wars, the brutality of empires — but we are part of it. If we don't feel our responsibility, which means being utterly responsible for ourselves, for what we do, what we think, how we behave, then it becomes rather hopeless, knowing what the world is, knowing that we cannot individually, separately, solve this problem of terrorism. That is the problem of governments, to see that its citizens are safe, protected, but they don't seem to care. If each government were really concerned to protect its own people, there would be no wars. But apparently governments have lost sanity too, they are only concerned with party politics, with their own power, position, prestige — you know all this, the whole game.

So can we, not admitting time, that is, tomorrow, the future, live in such a way that today is all-important? That means we have to become extraordinarily alert to our reactions, to our confusion — work like fury on ourselves. That is the only thing we can do apparently. And if we don't do that there is really no future for man. I do not know if you have followed some of the headlines in the newspapers — all this preparing for war. And if you are preparing for something, you are going to have it — like preparing a good dish. The ordinary people in the world apparently don't seem to care. Those who are intellectually, scientifically, involved in the production of armaments don't care. They are only interested in their careers, in their jobs, in their research; and those of us who are fairly ordinary people, so-called middle class, if we don't care at all, then we are really throwing in the sponge. The tragedy is that we don't seem to care. We don't get together, think together, work together. We are only too willing to join institutions, organizations, hoping they will stop wars, stop us butchering each other. They have never done it. Institutions, organizations will never stop any of this. It is the human heart, the human mind that is involved in this. Please, we are not talking rhetorically; we are facing something really very dangerous. We have met some of the prominent people who are involved in all this, and they don't care. But if we care and our daily life is lived rightly, if each one of us is aware of what we are doing daily, then I think there is some hope for the future.

Meeting Life

Question: Why do you waste your time preaching instead of helping the world in a practical way?

KRISHNAMURTI: Now, what do you mean by 'practical'? You mean bringing about a change in the world, a better economic adjustment, a better distribution of wealth, a better relationship — or, to put it more brutally, helping you to find a better job. You want to see a change in this world — every intelligent man does — and you want a method to bring about that change, and therefore you ask me why I waste my time preaching instead of doing something about it. Now, is what I am actually doing a waste of time? It would be a waste of time, would it not, if I introduced a new set of ideas to replace the old ideology, the old pattern. Perhaps that is what you want me to do. But instead of pointing out a so-called practical way to act, to live, to get a better job, to create a better world, is it not important to find out what are the impediments which actually prevent a real revolution — not a revolution of the left or the right, but a fundamental, radical revolution, not based on ideas? Because, as we have discussed it, ideals, beliefs, ideologies, dogmas, prevent action. There cannot be a world transformation, a revolution, as long as action is based on ideas because action then is merely reaction; therefore ideas become much more important than action, and that is precisely what is taking place in the world, isn't it? To act, we must discover the impediments that prevent action. But most of us don't want to act — that is our difficulty. We prefer to discuss, we prefer to substitute one ideology for another, and so we escape from action through ideology. Surely, that is very simple, is it not? The world at the present time is facing many problems; over-population, starvation, division of people into nationalities and classes, and so on. Why isn't there a group of people sitting together trying to solve the problems of nationalism? But if we try to become international while clinging to our nationality, we create another problem, and that is what most of us do. So you see that ideals are really preventing action. A statesman, an eminent authority, has said the world can be organized and all the people fed. Then why is it not done? Because of conflicting ideas, beliefs, and nationalisms. Therefore ideas are actually preventing the feeding of people, and most of us play with ideas and think we are tremendous revolutionaries, hypnotizing ourselves with such words as 'practical'. What is important is to free ourselves from ideas, from nationalisms, from all religious beliefs and dogmas, so that we can act, not according to a pattern or an ideology, but as needs demand; and, surely, to point out the hindrances and impediments that prevent such action is not a waste of time, is not a lot of hot air. What you are doing is obviously nonsense. Your ideas and beliefs, your political, economic, and religious panaceas, are actually dividing people and leading to war. It is only when the mind is free of idea and belief that it can act rightly. A man who is patriotic, nationalistic, can never know what it is to be brotherly, though he may talk about it; on the contrary, his actions, economically and in every direction, are conducive to war. So there can be right action and therefore radical, lasting transformation, only when the mind is free of ideas, not superficially, but fundamentally, and freedom from ideas can take place only through self-awareness and self-knowledge.

The Collected Works of J. Krishnamurti: vol. VI
Colombo, January 1, 1950

Question: Most of us are caught up in and are bored with the routine of our work, but our livelihood depends on it. Why can we not be happy in our work?

KRISHNAMURTI: Surely, modern civilization is making many of us do work which we as individuals do not like at all. Society as it is now constituted, being based on competition, ruthlessness, war, demands, let us say, engineers and scientists; they are wanted everywhere throughout the world because they can further develop the instruments of war and make the nation more efficient in its ruthlessness. So education is largely dedicated to building the individual into an engineer or a scientist, whether he is fit for it or not. The man who is being educated as an engineer may not really want to be one. He may want to be a painter, a musician, or who knows what else. But circumstances — education, family tradition, the demands of society, and so on — force him to specialize as an engineer. So we have created a routine in which most of us get caught, and then we are frustrated, miserable, unhappy for the rest of our lives. We all know this.

It is fundamentally a matter of education, is it not? And can we bring about a different kind of education in which each person, the teacher as well as the student, loves what he is doing? *Loves* — I mean exactly that word. But you cannot love what you are doing if you are all the time using it as a means to success, power, position, prestige.

Surely, as it is now constituted, society does produce individuals who are utterly bored, who are caught in the routine of what they are doing. So it will take a tremendous revolution, will it not, in education and in everything else, to bring about a totally different environment — an environment which will help the students, the children, to grow in that which they really love to do.

As things are now, we have to put up with routine, with boredom, and so we try to escape in various ways. We try to escape through amusements, through television or the radio, through books, through so-called religion, and so our lives become very shallow, empty, dull. This shallowness in turn breeds the acceptance of authority, which gives us a sense of universality, of power, position. We know all this in our hearts, but it is very difficult to break away from it all because to break away demands, not the usual sentimentality, but thought, energy, hard work.

So if you want to create a new world — and surely you must after these terrible wars, after the misery, the terrors that human beings have gone through — then there will have to be a religious revolution in each one of us, a revolution that will bring about a new culture and a totally new religion, which is not the religion of authority, of priestcraft, of dogma and ritual. To create a wholly different kind of society, there must be this religious revolution — that is, a revolution within the individual, and not the terrible outward bloodshed which only brings more tyranny, more misery and fear. If we are to create a new world — new in a totally different sense — then it must be our world, and not a German world or a Russian world or a Hindu world, for we are all human beings, and the earth is ours.

But unfortunately very few of us feel deeply about all this because it demands love, not sentimentality or emotionalism. Love is hard to find, and the man who is sentimentally emotional is generally cruel. To bring about a totally different culture, it seems to me that there must take place in each one of us this religious revolution, which means that there must be freedom, not only from all creeds and dogmas, but freedom from personal ambition and self-centred activity. Only then, surely, can there be a new world.

The Collected Works of J. Krishnamurti: vol. X
Hamburg, September 15, 1956

Question: My wife and I quarrel. We seem to like each other, but yet this wrangling goes on. We have tried several ways of putting an end to this ugliness, but we seem unable to be psychologically free of each other. What do you suggest?

KRISHNAMURTI: As long as there is dependency, there must be tension. If I depend on you as an audience in order to fulfil myself, in order to feel that I am somebody talking to a vast number of people, then I depend on you, I exploit you, you are necessary to me psychologically. This dependence is called love, and all our relationship is based on it. Psychologically I need you, and psychologically you need me. Psychologically you become important in my relationship with you because you fill my needs — not only physically, but also inwardly. Without you, I am lost, I am uncertain. I depend upon you; I love you. Whenever that dependence is questioned, there is uncertainty — and then I am afraid. And to cover up that fear, I resort to all kinds of subterfuges which will help me to get away from that fear. We know all this — we use property, knowledge, gods, illusions, relationship, as a means to cover our own emptiness, our own loneliness, and so these things become very important. The things which have become our escapes become extraordinarily valuable.

So as long as there is dependence, there must be fear. It is not love. You may call it love; you may cover it up with any pleasant sounding word. But actually, beneath it there is a void; there is the wound which cannot be healed by any method, which can only come to an end when you are conscious of it, aware of it, understand it. And there can be understanding only when you are not seeking an explanation. You see, the questioner demands an explanation; he wants words from me. And we are satisfied by words. The new explanation — if it is new — you will repeat. But the problem is still there; there will still be wrangling.

But when once we understand this process of dependence — the outward as well as the inward, the hidden dependencies, the psychological urgencies, the demand for the 'more' — when we understand those things, only then, surely, is there a possibility of love. Love is neither personal nor impersonal; it is a state of being. It is not of the mind; the mind cannot acquire it. You cannot practise love, or through meditation acquire it. It comes into being only when there is no fear, when this sense of anxiety, loneliness, has ceased, when there is no dependence or acquisition. And that comes only when we understand ourselves, when we are fully cognizant of our hidden motives, when the mind can delve into the depths of itself without seeking an answer, an explanation, when it is no longer naming.

Surely, one of our difficulties is, is it not, that most of us are satisfied with the superficialities of life — with explanations, chiefly. And we think we have solved all things by explaining them — which is the activity of the mind. As long as we can name, recognize, we think we have achieved something, and the moment there is the idea of no recognition, no naming, no explanation, then the mind gets confused. But only where there are no explanations, when the mind is not caught in words, is it possible for love to come into being.

The Collected Works of J. Krishnamurti: vol. VI
London, April 15, 1952

Question: Marriage is a necessary part of any organized society, but you seem to be against the institution of marriage. What do you say? Please also explain the problem of sex. Why has it become, next to war, the most urgent problem of our day?

KRISHNAMURTI: To ask a question is easy, but the difficulty is to look very carefully into the problem itself, which contains the answer. To understand this problem, we must see its enormous implications. That is difficult because our time is very limited and I shall have to be brief, and if you don't follow very closely, you may not be able to understand. Let us investigate the problem, not the answer, because the answer is in the problem, not away from it. The more I understand the problem, the clearer I see the answer. If you merely look for an answer, you will not find one because you will be seeking an answer away from the problem. Let us look at marriage, but not theoretically or as an ideal, which is rather absurd; don't let us idealize marriage, let us look at it as it is, for then we do something about it. If you make it rosy, then you can't act, but if you look at it and see it exactly as it is, then perhaps you will be able to act.

Now, what actually takes place? When one is young, the biological, sexual urge is very strong, and in order to set a limit to it you have the institution called marriage. There is the biological urge on both sides, so you marry and have children. You tie yourself to a man or to a woman for the rest of your life, and in doing so you have a permanent source of pleasure, a guaranteed security, with the result that you begin to disintegrate; you live in a cycle of habit, and habit is disintegration. To understand this biological, this sexual urge, requires a great deal of intelligence, but we are not educated to be intelligent. We merely get on with a man or a woman with whom we have to live. I marry at 20 or 25, and I have to live for the rest of my life with a woman whom I have not known. I have not known a thing about her, and yet you ask me to live with her for the rest of my life. Do you call that marriage? As I grow and observe, I find her to be completely different from me, her interests are different from mine; she is interested in clubs, I am interested in being very serious, or vice versa. And yet we have children — that is the most extraordinary thing. Sirs, don't look at the ladies and smile; it is your problem. So I have established a relationship the significance of which I do not know; I have neither discovered it nor understood it.

It is only for the very, very few who love that the married relationship has significance, and then it is unbreakable, then it is not mere habit or convenience, nor is it based on biological, sexual need. In that love, which is unconditional, the identities are fused, and in such a relationship there is a remedy, there is hope. But for most of you, the married relationship is not fused. To fuse the separate identities, you have to know yourself, and she has to know herself. That means to love. But there is no love, which is an obvious fact.

Love is fresh, new, not mere gratification, not mere habit. It is unconditional. You don't treat your husband or wife that way, do you? You live in your isolation, and she lives in her isolation, and you have established your habits of assured sexual pleasure. What happens to a man who has an assured income? Surely, he deteriorates. Have you not noticed it? Watch a man who has an assured income and you will soon see how rapidly his mind is withering away. He may have a big position, a reputation for cunning, but the full joy of life is gone out of him.

Similarly, you have a marriage in which you have a permanent source of pleasure, a habit without understanding, without love, and you are forced to live in that state. I am not saying what you should do, but look at the problem first. Do you think that is right? It does not mean that you must throw off your wife and pursue someone else. What does this relationship mean? Surely, to love is to be in communion with somebody, but are you in communion with your wife, except physically? Do you know her, except physically? Does she know you? Are you not both isolated, each pursuing his or her own interests, ambitions and needs, each seeking from the other gratification, economic or psychological security? Such a relationship is not a relationship at all — it is a mutually self-enclosing process of psychological, biological, and economic necessity — and the obvious result is conflict, misery, nagging, possessive fear, jealousy, and so on. Do you think such a relationship is productive of anything except ugly babies and an ugly civilization?

Therefore the important thing is to see the whole process, not as something ugly, but as an actual fact which is taking place under your very nose, and realizing that, what are you going to do? You cannot leave it at that, but because you do not want to look into it, you take to drink, to politics, to a lady around the corner, to anything that takes you away from the house and from that nagging wife or husband —

and you think you have solved the problem. That is your life, is it not? Therefore you have to do something about it, which means you have to face it, and that means, if necessary, breaking up; because, when a father and mother are constantly nagging and quarrelling with each other, do you think that has not an effect on the children?

So marriage as a habit, as a cultivation of habitual pleasure, is a deteriorating factor because there is no love in habit. Love is not habitual; love is something joyous, creative, new. Therefore habit is the contrary of love, but you are caught in habit, and naturally your habitual relationship with another is dead. So we come back again to the fundamental issue, which is that the reformation of society depends on you, not on legislation. Legislation can only make for further habit or conformity. Therefore you as a responsible individual in relationship have to do something — you have to act, and you can act only when there is an awakening of your mind and heart. I see some of you nodding your heads in agreement with me, but the obvious fact is that you don't want to take the responsibility for transformation, for change; you don't want to face the upheaval of finding out how to live rightly. And so the problem continues; you quarrel and carry on, and finally you die, and when you die somebody weeps, not for the other fellow, but for his or her own loneliness. You carry on unchanged, and you think you are human beings capable of legislation, of occupying high positions, talking about God, finding a way to stop wars, and so on. None of these things means anything because you have not solved any of the fundamental issues.

Then, the other part of the problem is sex and why sex has become so important. Why has this urge taken such a hold on you? Have you ever thought it out? You have not thought it out because you have just indulged; you have not searched out why there is this problem. Sirs, why is there this problem? And what happens when you deal with it by suppressing it completely — you know, the ideal of *brahmacharya*, and so on? What happens? It is still there. You resent anybody who talks about a woman, and you think that you can succeed in completely suppressing the sexual urge in yourself and solve your problem that way, but you are haunted by it. It is like living in a house and putting all your ugly things in one room, but they are still there. So discipline is not going to solve this problem — discipline being sublimation, suppression, substitution — because you have tried it, and that is not the way out. So what is the way out? The way out is to understand the problem, and to understand is not to condemn or justify. Let us look at it, then, in that way.

Why has sex become so important a problem in your life? Is not the sexual act, the feeling a way of self-forgetfulness? Do you understand what I mean? In that act there is complete fusion; at that moment there is complete cessation of all conflict; you feel supremely happy because you no longer feel the need as a separate entity, and you are not consumed with fear. That is, for a moment there is an ending of self-consciousness, and you feel the clarity of self-forgetfulness, the joy of self-abnegation. So sex has become important because in every other direction you are living a life of conflict, of self-aggrandizement, and frustration. Sirs, look at your lives — political social, religious — you are striving to become something. Politically you want to be somebody powerful, to have position, prestige. Don't look at somebody else, don't look at the ministers. If you were given all that, you would do the same thing. So politically you are striving to become somebody, you are expanding yourself, are you not? Therefore you are creating conflict; there is no denial, there is no abnegation of the 'me'. On the contrary, there is accentuation of the 'me'. The same process goes on in your relationship with things, which is ownership of property, and again in the religion that you follow. There is no meaning in what you are doing, in your religious practices. You just believe, you cling to labels, words. If you observe you will see that there, too, there is no freedom from the consciousness of the 'me' as the centre. Though your religion says, 'Forget yourself', your very process is the assertion of yourself, you are still the important entity. You may read the Gita or the Bible, but you are still the minister, you are still the exploiter, sucking the people and building temples.

So in every field, in every activity, you are indulging and emphasizing yourself, your importance, your prestige, your security. Therefore there is only one source of self-forgetfulness, which is sex, and that is why the woman or the man becomes all-important to you and why you must possess. So you build a society which enforces that possession, guarantees you that possession, and naturally sex becomes the all-important problem when everywhere else the self is the important thing. And do you think, sirs, that one can live in that state without contradiction, without misery, without frustration? But when there is honestly and sincerely no self-emphasis, whether in religion or in social activity, then sex has very little meaning. It is because you are afraid to be as nothing — politically, socially, religiously — that sex becomes a problem, but if in all these things you allowed yourself to diminish, to be the less, you would see that sex becomes no problem at all.

There is chastity only when there is love. When there is love, the problem of sex ceases; and without love, to pursue the ideal of *brahmacharya* is an absurdity because the ideal is unreal. The real is that which you are, and if you don't understand your own mind, the workings of your own mind, you will not understand sex because sex is a thing of the mind. The problem is not simple. It needs, not mere habit-forming practices, but tremendous thought and enquiry into your relationship with people, with property, and with ideas. Sir, it means you have to undergo strenuous searching of your heart and mind, thereby bringing a transformation within yourself. Love is chaste, and when there is love, and not the mere idea of chastity created by the mind, then sex has lost its problem and has quite a different meaning.

The Collected Works of J. Krishnamurti: vol. V
New Delhi, December 19, 1948

Question: What kind of education should my child have in order to face this chaotic world?

KRISHNAMURTI: This is really a vast question, isn't it, not to be answered in a couple of minutes. But perhaps we can put it briefly, and it may be gone into further afterwards.

The problem is not what kind of education the child should have but rather that the educator needs education, the parent needs education. (Murmur of laughter) No, please, this is not a clever remark for you to laugh at, be amused at. Do we not need a totally different kind of education? — not the mere cultivation of memory, which gives the child a technique, which will help him to get a job, a livelihood, but an education that will make him truly intelligent. Intelligence is the comprehension of the whole process, the total process of life, not knowledge of one fragment of life.

So the problem is really: Can we, the grown-up people, help the child to grow in freedom, in complete freedom? This does not mean allowing him to do what he likes, but can we help the child to understand what it is to be free because we understand ourselves what it is to be free?

Our education now is merely a process of conformity, helping the child to conform to a particular pattern of society in which he will get a job, become outwardly respectable, go to church, conform, and struggle until he dies. We do not help him to be free inwardly so that as he grows older, he is able to face all the complexities of life — which means helping him to have the capacity to think, not teaching him what to think. For this, the educator himself must be capable of freeing his own mind from all authority, from all fear, from all nationality, from the various forms of belief and tradition, so that the child understands — with your help, with your intelligence — what it is to be free, what it is to question, to enquire, and to discover.

But, you see, we do not want such a society; we do not want a different world. We want the repetition of the old world, only modified, made a little better, a little more polished. We want the child to conform totally, not to think at all, not to be aware, not to be inwardly clear — because if he is so inwardly clear, there is danger to all our established values. So what is really involved in this question is how to bring education to the educator. How can you and I — because we, the parents, the society, are the educators — how can you and I help to bring about clarity in ourselves so that the child may also be able to think freely, in the sense of having a still mind, a quiet mind, through which new things can be perceived and come into being?

This is really a very fundamental question. Why is it that we are being educated at all? Just for a job? Just to accept Catholicism or Protestanism, or communism or Hinduism? Just to conform to a certain tradition, to fit into a certain job? Or is education something entirely different? — not the cultivation of memory, but the process of understanding. Understanding does not come through analysis; understanding comes only when the mind is very quiet, unburdened, no longer seeking success and therefore being thwarted, afraid of failure. Only when the mind is still, only then is there a possibility of understanding, and having intelligence. Such education is the right kind of education, from which obviously other things follow.

But very few of us are interested in all that. If you have a child, you want him to have a job; that is all you are concerned with — what is going to happen to his future. Should the child inherit all the things that you have — the property, the values, the beliefs, the traditions — or must he grow in freedom, so as to discover for himself what is true? That can only happen if you yourself are not inheriting, if you yourself are free to enquire, to find out what is true.

The Collected Works of J. Krishnamurti: vol. IX
Amsterdam, May 19, 1955

Question: What is psychosomatic disease, and can you suggest ways to cure it?

KRISHNAMURTI: I do not think it is possible to find ways to cure psychosomatic disease, and perhaps the very search for a way to cure the mind is producing the disease. To find a way, or to practise a method, implies inhibiting, controlling, suppressing thought, which is not to understand the mind. It is fairly obvious that the mind does create disease in the physical organism. If you eat when you are angry, your tummy is upset; if you violently hate somebody, you have a physical disorder; if you restrict your mind to a particular belief, you become mentally or psychically neurotic, and it reacts upon the body. This is all part of the psychosomatic process. Of course, not all diseases are psychosomatic, but fear, anxiety and other disturbances of the psyche do produce physical diseases. So is it possible for the mind to be made healthy? Many of us are concerned with keeping the body healthy through right diet, and so on, which is essential; but very few are concerned with keeping the mind healthy, young, alert, vital, so that it does not deteriorate.

Now, if the mind is not to deteriorate, it must obviously never follow; it must be independent, free. But our education does not help us to be free; on the contrary, it helps us to fit into this deteriorating society; therefore the mind itself deteriorates. We are encouraged from childhood to be fearful, competitive, to think always about ourselves and our own security. Naturally, such a mind must be in everlasting conflict, and that conflict does produce physical effects. What is important, then, is to discover and understand for ourselves, through our own vigilant watchfulness, the whole process of conflict and not depend on any psychologist or guru. To follow a guru is to destroy your mind. You follow him because you want what you think he has; therefore you have set going a process of deterioration. The effort to be somebody, mundanely or spiritually, is another form of deterioration, because such effort always brings anxiety; it produces fear, frustration, making the mind unhealthy, which in turn affects the body. I think this is fairly simple. But to look to another for the cure of the mind is part of the process of deterioration.

The Collected Works of J. Krishnamurti: vol. IX
Bombay, March 28, 1956

Question: My body and my mind seem to be made up of deep-rooted urges and conscious and unconscious fears; I watch the mind, but often it is as if these basic fears overpower me. What am I to do?

KRISHNAMURTI: Sir, let us find out what we mean by fear. What is fear? Fear exists only in relation to something. It is not something by itself. It is only in relation to something — to what you might say of me, to what the public may think of me, to the loss of a job, in having security in my old age, or the fear of the mother's or father's death, or God knows what. It is the fear of something.

Now, how am I to be free from fear? Will discipline of any kind dispel fear? Discipline is resistance, the cultivation of resistance to learn. Will that free the mind from fear? Or will it only hold it away from it — like building a wall, but on the other side there is always fear? Fear obviously cannot be got rid of by resistance, by the cultivation of courage because the very nature of courage is the opposite of fear, and when the mind is caught up in fear and courage, there is no solution but the cultivation of resistance, so there is no overcoming of fear through cultivation of courage.

How am I to get rid of fear? Please follow this, sirs. This is our problem, yours and mine, of every human being who wishes to be free from fear because if I can be free from fear, then the 'me', the self which is creating so much mischief, so much misery in the world can disappear. Is not the self, in its very nature, the cause of fear? Because I want to be secure, if I am not economically secure, I want to be secure politically, socially, in name, I want to be secure in the hereafter, I want to have God's assurance, to pat me on the back and say, 'You will have a better chance next life'; I want somebody to tell me, to encourage me, to give me shelter, refuge. So, as long as I am seeking security in any form, there must be fear, from which all the basic urges spring. So if I can understand what fear is, perhaps then there may be a release from that constant choice.

How am I to understand what fear is? How am I — without disciplining, without resisting, without running away from it, without creating other illusions, other problems, other systems of gurus, of philosophers — to really face it, to understand it, to be free of it and go beyond it? I can only understand fear when I am not running away from it, when I am not resisting it. So we have to find out what this entity is that is resisting. Who is the 'I' that is resisting fear? Do you understand, sirs? That is, I am afraid; I am afraid of what the public might say about me because I want to be a very respectable person; I want to succeed in the world; I want to have a name, position, authority. So one side of me is pursuing that, and inwardly, I know that anything I do will lead to frustration, that what I want to do will block me. So there are two processes working in me — one, the entity that wants to achieve, to become respectable, to become successful; and the other, the entity that is always afraid that I might not achieve.

So there are two processes in myself operating, two desires, two pursuits — one that says, 'I want to be happy', and the other that knows that there may not be happiness in the world. I want to be rich, and at the same time I see millions of poor people, and yet my ambition is to be rich. So long as the desire for security confronts me, drives me, there is no release; at the same time there is in me compassion, love, sensitivity. There is a battle going on endlessly and that battle projects, becomes antisocial, and so on and so on. So what am I to do? How am I to be free from this battle, from this inward conflict?

If I can observe one process alone and not cultivate the dual process, then there is a possibility of dealing with it. That is, if I can observe fear in itself and not cultivate virtue, not cultivate courage, then I can deal with fear. That is, if I know 'what is' and not 'what should be', then I can deal with 'what is'. With most of us we do not know 'what is', for most of us are concerned with 'what should be'. This 'should be' creates the duality. 'What is' never creates duality. 'What should be' brings about the conflict, the duality.

So can I observe 'what is' without the conflict of the opposite, can I look at 'what is' without any resistance? Because the very resistance creates the opposite, does it not? That is, when I am afraid, can I look at it without creating resistance? Because the moment I create resistance against it, I have already brought into being another conflict. Can I look at 'what is' without any resistance? If I can do that, then I can begin to deal with fear.

Now, what is fear? Is fear a word, an idea, a thought, or an actuality? Does fear come into being because of the word 'fear', or is that fear independent of the word? Please, sir, think it out with me. Don't get tired. Don't let your minds go off. Because, if you are really concerned with the problem of fear, which you are, which every human being is — fear of death, fear of your grandfather or grandmother dying — since you are burdened with that extraordinary darkness, should you not go into the problem and not just push it aside? If we go into this problem carefully, we see that as long as we are creating a resistance against fear in any form, running away from it, building barriers against it like cultivating courage and so on, that very resistance brings about conflict which is the conflict of the opposites. And through the conflict of the opposites, we will never come to an understanding.

The idea that conflict between thesis and antithesis will bring about a synthesis is not true. What brings about understanding is comprehending the fact of 'what is' and not by creating the opposite. So can I face fear, look at fear without resisting, without running away from it? Now, what is this entity that is looking at fear? When I say I am afraid, what is the 'I' and what is the 'fear'? Are they two different states, are they two different processes? Am I different from the fear which the 'I' feels? If I am different from the fear, then I can operate on fear; then I can change it; then I can resist it, push it away. But if I am not different from fear, then is there not a different action altogether?

Is this a little bit abstract and too difficult for you, sirs? Please let us go into it. Listen to it, just listen; don't bother to argue because by listening, not throwing up arguments, by just listening, you can comprehend what I am talking about.

As long as I am resisting fear, there is no freedom from fear but only further conflict, further misery. When I do not resist, there is only fear. Then is fear different from the observer, the 'me' that says, 'I am afraid'? What is this 'me' that says, 'I am afraid'? Is not the 'me' composed of that feeling which I call fear? Is not the 'me' the feeling of fear? If there was no feeling of fear, there would be no 'me'. So the 'me' and the fear are one. There is no 'me' apart from fear, so fear is 'me'. So there is only fear.

Now, there is the enquiry, Is fear merely the word? Does the word 'fear', the idea, the symbol, the state — is that created by the mind independent of the fact? Please listen. Fear is 'me'; there is no independent 'I' apart from me. The man, the 'I' says, 'I am greedy'; the authority is the 'I'. The quality is not different from the 'I'. So long as the 'I' says, 'I must be free from greed', it is making an effort, it is struggling. But that very 'I' is still greedy because it wants to be non-greedy. Similarly, when the 'I' says, 'I must be free from fear', it is cultivating a resistance, and so there is conflict, and it is never free from fear. So there is only freedom from fear when I recognize the fact, when there is an understanding of the fact that the fear is the 'I', and the 'I' cannot do anything about fear. Please see the 'I' that says, 'I am afraid, I must do something about fear'. As long as it is acting upon fear, it only creates resistance and therefore increases further conflict. But when I recognize that the fear is 'me', then there is no action of the 'I'; it is only then that there is freedom from fear.

You see, we are so accustomed to do something about fear, about an urge, about a sexual urge, that we always act upon it as though that urge is independent of 'me'. So as long as we are treating the desire as independent of 'me' there must be conflict. There is no desire without 'me'. I am the desire; the two things are not separate. Please see this. It is really a tremendous experience when there is this feeling that fear is 'me', that greed is 'me', that it is not apart from 'me'.

There is no thought without the thinker. As long there is the thought there is the thinker. The thinker is not separate from thought, but thought creates the thinker, puts him apart because thought is everlastingly seeking permanency and so creates the 'I' as a permanent entity, the 'I' that controls thought. But without thought there is no 'I'; when you don't think, when you don't recognize, when you don't distinguish, is there the 'I'? Is there the 'me'? The very process of thinking creates the 'me'; then the 'me' operates on thought. So the struggle goes on indefinitely.

If there is the intention to be free from fear completely, then there must be the recognition of the truth that fear is 'me', that there is no fear apart from 'me'. That is the fact. When you are faced with a fact then there is action — an action which is not brought about by the conscious mind, an action which is the truth, not of choice, not of resistance. Then only is there a possibility of freeing the mind from every kind of fear.

The Collected Works of J. Krishnamurti: vol. VII
Bombay, February 15, 1953

Question: *I am in conflict and suffering. For thousands of years we have been told of the causes of suffering and the way of its cessation, and yet we are where we are today. Is it possible to end this suffering?*

KRISHNAMURTI: I wonder how many of us are aware that we are suffering. Are you aware, not theoretically but actually, that you are in conflict? And if you are, what do you do? You try to escape from it, don't you? The moment one is aware of this conflict and suffering, one tries to forget it in intellectual pursuits, in work, or in seeking enjoyment, pleasure. One seeks an escape from suffering, and all escapes are the same, are they not, whether they are cultured or crude. What do we mean by conflict? When are you aware that you are in conflict? Conflict arises, surely, when there is the consciousness of the ‘me’. There is awareness of the conflict only when the ‘me’ suddenly becomes conscious of itself; otherwise you lead a monotonous, superficial, dull, routine life, don’t you? You are aware of yourself only when there is conflict, and as long as everything is moving smoothly without a contradiction, without a frustration, there is no consciousness of yourself in action. As long as I am not pushed around, as long as I am getting what I want, I am not in conflict, but the moment I am blocked, I am aware of myself and become miserable. In other words, conflict arises only when there is a sense of ‘myself’ facing a frustration in action. So what do we want? We want to have an action which is constantly self-fulfilling, without frustration; that is, we want to live without being blocked. In other words, we want our desires fulfilled, and as long as those desires are not fulfilled, there is conflict, there is contradiction. So our problem is how to fulfil, how to achieve self-fulfilment without frustration. I want to possess something — property, a person, a title, or what you will — and if I can get it and go on getting what I want, then I am happy, there is no contradiction. So what we are seeking is self-fulfilment, and as long as we can achieve that fulfilment, there is no friction.

Now, the question is, is there such a thing as self-fulfilment? That is, can I achieve something, become something, realize something? And in that desire, is there not a constant battle? That is, as long as I crave to become something, to achieve something, to fulfil myself, there must be frustration, there must be fear, there must be conflict; and therefore, is there such a thing as self-fulfilment? What do we mean by self-fulfilment? By self-fulfilment we mean self-expansion — the ‘me’ becoming wider, greater, more important; the ‘me’ becoming the governor, the executive, the bank manager, and so on. Now, if you go into it a little more deeply, you will see that as long as there is this action of the self, that is, as long as there is self-consciousness in action, there must be frustration; therefore there must be suffering. Hence our problem is not how to overcome suffering, how to put aside conflict, but to understand the nature of the self, the 'me'. I hope I am not making this too complicated. If we merely try to overcome conflict, try to put sorrow aside, we do not understand the nature of the creator of sorrow.

As long as thought is concerned with its own improvement, its own transformation, its own advancement, there must be conflict and contradiction. So we come back to the obvious fact that conflict, suffering, will exist as long as I do not understand myself. Therefore to understand oneself is more important than to know how to overcome sorrow and conflict. We can go further into all this later. But to escape from sorrow through rituals, through amusements, through beliefs, or any other form of distraction is to take your thought further and further away from the central issue, which is to understand yourself. To understand suffering, there must be cessation of all escapes, for only then are you able to face yourself in action; and in understanding yourself in action — which is relationship — you will find a way of completely freeing thought from all conflict and living in a state of happiness, of reality.

The Collected Works of J. Krishnamurti: vol. V
New Delhi, November 14, 1948

Question: *You have said that all urges are in essence the same. Do you mean to say that the urge of the man who pursues God is no different from the urge of the man who pursues women or who loses himself in drink?*

KRISHNAMURTI: All urges are not similar, but they are all urges. You may have an urge towards God, and I may have an urge to get drunk, but we are both compelled, urged — you in one direction, I in another. Your direction is respectable, mine is not; on the contrary, I am antisocial. But the hermit, the monk, the so-called religious person whose mind is occupied with virtue, with God, is essentially the same as the man whose mind is occupied with business, with women, or with drink, because both are occupied. Do you understand? The one has sociological value, while the other, the man whose mind is occupied with drink, is socially unfit. So you are judging from the social point of view, are you not? The man who retires into a monastery and prays from morning till night, doing some gardening for a certain period of the day, whose mind is wholly occupied with God, with self-castigation, self-discipline, self-control — him you regard as a very holy person, a most extraordinary man. Whereas the man who goes after business, who manipulates the stock exchange and is occupied all the time with making money, of him you say, 'Well, he is just an ordinary man like the rest of us'. But they are both occupied. To me, what the mind is occupied with is not important. A man whose mind is occupied with God will never find God because God is not something to be occupied with; it is the unknown, the immeasurable. You cannot occupy yourself with God. That is a cheap way of thinking of God.

What is significant is not with what the mind is occupied but the fact of its occupation, whether it be with the kitchen, with the children, with amusement, with what kind of food you are going to have, or with virtue, with God. And must the mind be occupied? Do you follow? Can an occupied mind ever see anything new, anything except its own occupation? And what happens to the mind if it is not occupied? Do you understand? Is there a mind if there is no occupation? The scientist is occupied with his technical problems, with his mechanics, with his mathematics, as the housewife is occupied in the kitchen or with the baby. We are all so frightened of not being occupied, frightened of the social implications. If one were not occupied, one might discover oneself as one is, so occupation becomes an escape from what one is.

So, must the mind be everlastingly occupied? And is it possible to have no occupation of the mind? Please, I am putting to you a question to which there is no answer because you have to find out, and when you do find out, you will see the extraordinary thing happen.

It is very interesting to find out for yourself how your mind is occupied. The artist is occupied with his art, with his name, with his progress, with the mixing of colours, with fame, with notoriety; the man of knowledge is occupied with his knowledge; and a man who is pursuing self-knowledge is occupied with his self-knowledge, trying like a little ant to be aware of every thought, every movement. They are all the same. It is only the mind that is totally unoccupied, completely empty — it is only such a mind that can receive something new, in which there is no occupation. But that new thing cannot come into being as long as the mind is occupied.

The Collected Works of J. Krishnamurti: vol. IX
Ojai, August 14, 1955

Question: *When we die, are we reborn on this earth, or do we pass on into some other world?*

KRISHNAMURTI: This question interests all of us, the young and the old, does it not? So I am going into it rather deeply, and I hope you will be good enough to follow, not just the words, but the actual experience of what I am going to discuss with you.

We all know that death exists, especially the older people, and also the young who observe it. The young say, 'Wait until it comes and we'll deal with it'; and as the old are already near death, they have recourse to various forms of consolation.

Please follow and apply this to yourselves; don't put it off on somebody else. Because you know you are going to die, you have theories, about it, don't you? You believe in God, you believe in resurrection, or in karma and reincarnation; you say that you will be reborn here or in another world. Or you rationalize death, saying that death is inevitable, it happens to everybody; the tree withers away, nourishing the soil, and a new tree comes up. Or else you are too occupied with your daily worries, anxieties, jealousies, envies, with your competition and your wealth, to think about death at all. But it is in your mind; consciously or unconsciously it is there.

First of all, can you be free of the beliefs, the rationalities, or the indifference that you have cultivated towards death? Can you be free of all that now? Because what is important is to enter the house of death while living, while fully conscious, active, in health, and not wait for the coming of death, which may carry you off instantaneously through an accident, or through a disease that slowly makes you unconscious. When death comes, it must be an extraordinary moment which is as vital as living.

Now, can I, can you, enter the house of death while living? That is the problem — not whether there is reincarnation, or whether there is another world where you will be reborn, which is all so immature, so infantile. A man who lives never asks, 'what is living?' and he has no theories about living. It is only the half-alive who talk about the purpose of life.

So, can you and I while living, conscious, active, with all our capacities, whatever they be, know what death is? And is death then different from living? To most of us, living is a continuation of that which we think is permanent. Our name, our family, our property, the things in which we have a vested interest economically and spiritually, the virtues that we have cultivated, the things that we have acquired emotionally — all of that we want to continue. And the moment which we call death is a moment of the unknown; therefore we are frightened, so we try to find a consolation, some kind of comfort; we want to know if there is life after death, and a dozen other things. Those are all irrelevant problems; they are problems for the lazy, for those who do not want to find out what death is while living. So, can you and I find out?

What is death? Surely, it is the complete cessation of everything that you have known. If it is not the cessation of everything you have known, it is not death. If you know death already, then you have nothing to be frightened of. But do you know death? That is, can you while living put an end to this everlasting struggle to find in the impermanent something that will continue? Can you know the unknowable, that state which we call death, while living? Can you put aside all the descriptions of what happens after death which you have read in books, or which your unconscious desire for comfort dictates, and taste or experience that state, which must be extraordinary, now? If that state can be experienced now, then living and dying are the same.

So can I, who have vast education, knowledge, who have had innumerable experiences, struggles, loves, hates — can that 'I' come to an end? The 'I' is the recorded memory of all that, and can that 'I' come to an end? Without being brought to an end by an accident, by a disease, can you and I while sitting here know that end? Then you will find that you will no longer ask foolish questions about death and continuity — whether there is a world hereafter. Then you will know the answer for yourself because that which is unknowable will have come into being. Then you will put aside the whole rigmarole of reincarnation, and the many fears — the fear of living and the fear of dying, the fear of growing old and inflicting on others the trouble of looking after you, the fear of loneliness and dependency — will all have come to an end. These are not vain words. It is only when the mind ceases to think in terms of its own continuity that the unknowable comes into being.

The Collected Works of J. Krishnamurti: vol. IX
Ojai, August 21, 1955

Question: *I pray to God, and my prayers are answered. Is this not proof of the existence of God?*

KRISHNAMURTI: If you have proof of the existence of God, then it is not God (Laughter) because proof is of the mind. How can the mind prove or disprove God? Therefore your God is a projection of the mind according to your satisfaction, appetite, happiness, pleasure, or fear. Such a thing is not God but merely a creation of thought, a projection of the known, which is past. What is known is not God, though the mind may look for it, may be active in the search for God.

The questioner says that his prayers are answered and asks if this is not proof of the existence of God. Do you want proof of love? When you love somebody, do you seek proof? If you demand proof of love, is that love? If you love your wife, your child, and you want proof, then love is surely a bargain. So your prayer to God is merely bargaining. (Laughter) Don't laugh it off, look at it seriously, as a fact. The questioner approaches what he calls God through supplication and petition. You cannot find reality through sacrifice, through duty, through responsibility, because these are means to an end, and the end is not different from the means. The means are the end.

The other part of the question is, 'I pray to God, and my prayers are answered'. Let us examine that. What do you mean by prayer? Do you pray when you are joyous, when you are happy, when there is no confusion, no misery? You pray when there is misery, when there is disturbance, fear, turmoil, and your prayer is supplication, petition. When you are in misery, you want somebody to help you out, a higher entity to give you a helping hand, and that process of supplication in different forms is called prayer. So what happens? You put out your begging bowl to someone; it does not matter who it is — an angel, or your own projection whom you call God. The moment you beg, you have something — but whether that something is real or not is a different question. You want your confusion, your miseries solved, so you get out your traditional phrases, you turn on your devotion, and the constant repetition obviously makes the mind quiet. But that is not quietness — the mind is merely dulled and put to sleep. In that induced quiet, when there is supplication, there is an answer. But it is not at all an answer from God — it is from your own ornamental projection. Here is the answer to the question. But you do not want to enquire into all this, that is why the question is put. Your prayer is supplication — you are only concerned to get a response to your prayer because you want to be free from trouble. Something is gnawing at your heart, and by praying, you make yourself dull and quiet. In that artificial quietness there is a response — obviously satisfying, otherwise you would reject it. Your prayer is satisfying, and therefore it is what you yourself have created. It is your own projection that helps you out — that is one type of prayer. Then there is the deliberative type of prayer to make the mind quiet, receptive and open. How can the mind be open when it is conditioned by tradition, the background of the past? Openness implies understanding, the capacity to follow the imponderable. When the mind is held, tethered to a belief, it cannot be open. When it is deliberately opened, obviously any answer it receives is a projection of itself. Only when the mind is unconditioned, when it knows how to deal with each problem as it arises — only then is there no longer a problem. As long as the background continues, it must create a problem; as long as there is continuity, there must be ever-increasing turmoil and misery. Receptivity is the capacity to be open, without condemnation or justification, to 'what is'; and it is that from which you try to escape through prayer.

The Collected Works of J. Krishnamurti: vol. VI
Colombo, January 8, 1950

Question: *In moments of great anguish and despair, I surrender without effort to Him, without knowing Him. That dispels my despair; otherwise, I would be destroyed. What is this surrender, and is this a wrong process?*

KRISHNAMURTI: A mind that deliberately surrenders itself to something unknown is adopting a wrong process, like a man who deliberately cultivates love, humility, when he has no love, no humility. When I am violent, if I am trying to become non-violent, I am still violent. If I am practising humility, is it humility? It is only respectability, it is not humility. You see the truth of this, sirs? Don't smile and say how clever the statement is. It is not clever. A man who is deliberately persuading himself into being good, who is surrendering himself to something which he calls God, or to Him, does so deliberately, voluntarily, through an action of will. Such a surrender is not surrender; it is self-forgetfulness, it is a replacement, a substitute, an escape, it is like mesmerizing oneself, like taking a drug, or like repeating words without meaning.

I think there is a surrender which is not deliberate, which is totally unasked, undemanded. When the mind demands something, it is not surrender. When the mind demands peace, when it says, 'I love God, and I pursue the love of God', it is not love. All the deliberate activities of the mind are the continuance of the mind, and that which has continuity is in time. It is only in the cessation of time that there can be the being of reality. The mind cannot surrender.

All that the mind can do is to be still, but that stillness cannot come into being if there is despair or if there is hope. If you understand the process of despair, if the mind sees the whole significance of despair, you will see the truth of it. There is bound to be despair when you want something and when you cannot get what you want — it may be a car, it may be a woman, it may be God; they are all of the same quality. The moment you want something, the very wanting is the beginning of despair. Despair means frustration. You would be satisfied if you would get what you want, and because you cannot get what you want, you say, 'I must surrender to God'. If you got what you wanted, you would be perfectly satisfied; only that satisfaction comes to an end soon, and you seek another thing. So you change the object of your satisfaction constantly; this brings with it its own reward, its own pains, its own sufferings, its own pleasure.

If you understand that desire of any kind brings with it frustration, despair, and so the dual conflict of hope, if you really see the fact of that, if without saying, 'How am I to be in that state?' you just see that desire makes for pain, then the very seeing of it is the silencing of desire. Being aware choicelessly, purely, simply, that the mind is noisy, that the mind is in constant movement, in constant struggle, that very awareness brings about the ending of that noise choicelessly. Awareness is the important thing, not the dispelling of despair, not the silence. Pure intelligence is that state of mind in which there is awareness, in which there is no choice, in which the mind is silent. In that state of silence there is 'being' only; then that reality, that astounding creativity without time comes into being.

The Collected Works of J. Krishnamurti: vol. VIII
Bombay, February 10, 1954

Question: *What, according to you, is true meditation?*

KRISHNAMURTI: Now, what is the purpose of meditation? And what do we mean by meditation? I do not know if you have meditated, so let us experiment together to find out what is true meditation. Don't listen merely to my expression of it, but together we'll find out and experience what is true meditation. Because meditation is important, isn't it? If you do not know what is right meditation, there is no self-knowledge, and without knowing yourself, meditation has no meaning. To sit in a corner or walk about in the garden or in the street and try to meditate has no meaning. That only leads to a peculiar concentration, which is exclusion. I'm sure some of you have tried all those methods. That is, you try to concentrate on a particular object, try to force the mind, when it is wandering all over the place, to be concentrated; and when that fails, you pray.

So if one really wants to understand what is right meditation, one must find out what are the false things which we have called meditation. Obviously, concentration is not meditation because, if you observe, in the process of concentration there is exclusion, and therefore there is distraction. You are trying to concentrate on something, and your mind is wandering off towards something else, and there is this constant battle going on to be fixed on one point while the mind refuses and wanders off. And so we spend years trying to concentrate, to learn concentration, which is mistakenly called meditation.

Then there is the question of prayer. Prayer obviously produces results; otherwise millions wouldn't pray. And in praying, obviously the mind is made quiet; by constant repetition of certain phrases, the mind does become quiet. And in that quietness there is a certain intimation, certain perceptions, certain responses. But that is still a part of the trick of the mind because, after all, through a form of mesmerism you can make the mind very quiet. And in that quietness there are certain hidden responses arising from the unconscious and from outside the consciousness. But it is still a state in which there is no understanding.

And meditation is not devotion — devotion to an idea, to a picture, to a principle — because the things of the mind are still idolatrous. One may not worship a statue, considering it idolatrous and silly, superstitious; but one does worship, as most people do, the things in the mind — and that is also idolatrous. And to be devoted to a picture or an idea, to a Master, is not meditation. Obviously, it's a form of escape from oneself. It's a very comforting escape, but it's still an escape.

And this constant striving to become virtuous, to acquire virtue through discipline, through careful examination of oneself, and so on, is obviously not meditation either. Most of us are caught in these processes, and since they do not give understanding of ourselves, they are not the way of right meditation. After all, without understanding yourself, what basis have you for right thinking? All that you will do without that understanding of yourself is to conform to the background, to the response of your conditioning. And such response to the conditioning is not meditation. But to be aware of those responses, that is, to be aware of the movements of thought and feeling without any sense of condemnation so that the movements of the self, the ways of the self, are completely understood — that way is the way of right meditation.

Meditation is not a withdrawal from life. Meditation is a process of understanding oneself. And when one begins to understand oneself, not only the conscious, but all the hidden parts of oneself as well, then there comes tranquillity. A mind that is made still through meditation, through compulsion, through conformity, is not still. It is a stagnant mind. It is not a mind that is alert, passive, capable of creative receptivity. Meditation demands constant watchfulness, constant awareness of every word, every thought and feeling which reveals the state of our own being, the hidden as well as the superficial; and as that is arduous, we escape into every kind of comforting, deceptive thing and call it meditation.

If one can see that self-knowledge is the beginning of meditation, then the problem becomes extraordinarily interesting and vital. Because, after all, if there is no self-knowledge, you may practise what you call meditation and still be attached to your principles, to your family, to your property; or giving up your property, you may be attached to an idea and be so concentrated on it that you create more and more of that idea. Surely, that is not meditation. So self-knowledge is the beginning of meditation; without self-knowledge there is no meditation. And as one goes deeper into the question of self-knowledge, not only does the upper mind become tranquil, quiet, but the different layers of the hidden are revealed. When the superficial mind is quiet, then the unconscious, the hidden layers of consciousness project themselves; they reveal their content; they give their intimations so that the whole process of one's being is completely understood.

So the mind becomes extremely quiet — is quiet. It is not made quiet, it is not compelled to be quiet by a reward, by fear. Then there is a silence in which reality comes into being. But that silence is not Christian silence or Hindu silence or Buddhist silence. That silence is silence, not named. Therefore if you follow the path of Christian silence or Hindu or Buddhist, you will never be silent. Therefore a man who would find reality must abandon his conditioning completely — whether Christian, Hindu, Buddhist, or of any other group. Merely to strengthen the background through meditation, through conformity, brings about stagnation of the mind, dullness of the mind; and I'm not at all sure that's not what most of us want, because it's so much easier to create a pattern and follow it. But to be free of the background demands constant watchfulness in relationship.

And when once that silence is, then there is an extraordinary, creative state — not that you must write poems, paint pictures; you may or you may not. But that silence is not to be pursued, copied, imitated — then it ceases to be silence. You cannot come to it through any path. It comes into being only when the ways of the self are understood, and the self, with all its activities and mischief, comes to an end. That is, when the mind ceases to create, then there is creation. Therefore the mind must become simple, must become quiet, must be quiet — the 'must' is wrong; to say the mind must be quiet implies compulsion. And the mind is quiet only when the whole process of the self has come to an end. When all the ways of the self are understood, and therefore the activities of the self have come to an end — then only is there silence. That silence is true meditation, and in that silence the eternal comes into being.

The Collected Works of J. Krishnamurti: vol. V
London, October 23, 1949

Question: *Of all the spiritual teachers, you are the only one I know of who does not offer a system of meditation for the attainment of inner peace. We all agree that inner peace is necessary, but how can we attain it without practising a technique, whether of Eastern yoga or Western psychology?*

KRISHNAMURTI: Isn't it too bad that there are teachers, spiritual teachers and followers? The moment you have a teacher and you become the follower, have you not destroyed that flame which must constantly be kept alive if you are to find out, to discover? When you look to a teacher to help you, does not the teacher become more important than the truth you are seeking? So let us put aside the teacher-and-follower attitude; let us get it out of our systems completely and regard the problem itself as it is affecting each one of us. No teacher can help you to find truth, obviously; one has to find it within oneself; one has to go through the pain, the suffering, the enquiry; one has to discover and understand things for oneself. But in becoming the follower of a particular teacher, have you not cultivated inertia, laziness, is there not a darkening of the mind? And, of course, the various teachers with their various groups are in contradiction, competing with each other, doing propaganda — you know all the nonsense round it.

So the whole question of followers and teachers is ridiculous and childish. What is important in the question is this: Is there a method, whether Eastern or Western, to attain peace? If peace is attained through practising a certain method, that which you have attained and which you call peace is no longer a living quality; it is a dead thing. You know by formulation what peace should be, and you have laid down a path which you follow towards it. Surely, that peace is a projection of your own desire, is it not? Therefore it is no longer peace. It is what you want, a thing opposite to that which you are. I am in a state of conflict, of misery, of contradiction; I am unhappy, violent, and I want a refuge, a state in which I shall not be disturbed. So I go to various teachers, guides; I read books, practise disciplines which promise what I want; I suppress, control, conform in order to gain peace. And is that peace? Surely, peace is not a thing to be sought after — it comes. It is a by-product, not an end in itself. It comes when I am beginning to understand the whole process of myself, my contradictions, desires, ambitions, pride. But if I make of peace an end in itself, then I live in a state of stagnation. And is that peace?

So as long as I am seeking peace through a system, a method, a technique, I shall have peace, but it will be the peace of conformity, the peace of death. And that is what most of us want. I have had a glimmer of something, an experience which cannot be put into words, and I want to live in that state; I want it to continue; I want an absolute reality. There may be an absolute reality, or there may be experiences of greater and greater significance, but if I cling to one or the other, am I not cultivating slow death? And death is not peace. So I cannot possibly imagine what peace is in this state of confusion, in this state of conflict. What I can imagine is the opposite, and that which is opposite to what I am is not peace. So a technique merely helps me to obtain something which is the opposite of what I am, and without understanding what I am — going into it completely, not only at the conscious, but also at the unconscious levels — without understanding the whole process of myself, merely to seek peace has very little significance.

You see, most of us are lazy; we are so inert; we want teachers, monasteries to help us; we do not want to find out for ourselves through our own constant awareness, through our own enquiry, through our own experience, however vague, however subtle, elusive. So we join churches, groups, we become followers of this or that — which means there is a struggle on one side, and the cultivation of inertia on the other. But if one really wishes to find out, experience directly — and we can discuss what that experiencing is at another time — then surely it is imperative that one put aside all these things and understand oneself. Self-knowledge is the beginning of wisdom, and that alone can bring peace.

The Collected Works of J. Krishnamurti: vol. VII
Ojai, August 10, 1952

Question: *Thought goes on and on and on, all the time, endlessly. How is it possible to put a stop to it?*

KRISHNAMURTI: If I say, 'I don't know', what will you do? I really do not know. Sir, listen carefully to what is being said. So many ways have been tried — going to a monastery; identifying ourselves with some image, theory, or concept; through discipline, meditation, forcing, suppressing, trying to put an end to thought. Man has tried everything that is possible, tortured himself in a thousand different ways because he realizes that to think is to be full of sorrow. How is it to be done? There are several things involved. The moment you make an effort to stop it, then it becomes a problem. There is a contradiction. You want to stop it, and it keeps on and on and on. That very contradiction breeds conflict; all contradictions breed conflict. So what have you done? You have not ended thought but you have introduced a new problem, which is conflict. Any effort to stop thinking only feeds, gives more energy to, thinking. You know very well you have to think. You have to exercise every energy that you have to think clearly, spotlessly, to think sanely, rationally, logically. Yet you know that sane, rational, logical thinking does not stop thought. It goes on and on.

What are you to do? You know that any form of repression, any form of discipline, suppression, resistance, or conformity to an idea that you must stop thinking is a waste. You put all that aside. Have you? If you have, then what will you do? You will do absolutely nothing! First you think you must stop it. That is an idea and behind that there is a motive. You want to stop it because thought has not solved the problem. So can the mind — not just a part of it, a certain fragment of it, but the totality of the mind, in which is included the nerves, the brain, the feeling, everything — can the mind realize that it can do nothing about it; and then will it go on? You will find it will not go on.

The Collected Works of J. Krishnamurti: vol. XVI
Saanen, July 19, 1966

Question: *What is this self-knowledge of which you speak, and how can I acquire it? What is the starting point?*

KRISHNAMURTI: Now, please listen carefully because you have extraordinary ideas about self-knowledge — that to have self-knowledge you must practise, you must meditate, you must do all kinds of things. It is very simple, sir. The first step is the last step in self-knowledge, the beginning is the end. The first step is what matters because self-knowledge is not something you can learn from another. No one can teach you self-knowledge, you have to find out for yourself; it must be your own discovery, and that discovery is not something tremendous, fantastic, it is very simple. After all, to know yourself is to watch your behaviour, your words, what you do in your everyday relationships, that is all. Begin with that and you will see how extraordinarily difficult it is to be aware, just to watch the manner of your behaviour, the words you use to your servant, to your boss, the attitude you have with regard to people, to ideas, and to things. Just watch your thoughts, your motives, in the mirror of relationship, and you will see that the moment you watch, you want to correct, you say, 'This is good, that is bad, I must do this and not that'. When you see yourself in the mirror of relationship, your approach is one of condemnation or justification, therefore you distort what you see. Whereas, if you simply observe in that mirror your attitude with regard to people, to ideas, and to things, if you just see the fact without judgement, without condemnation or acceptance, then you will find that that very perception has its own action. That is the beginning of self-knowledge.

To watch yourself, to observe what you do, what you think, what your motives and incentives are, and yet not condemn or justify, is an extraordinarily difficult thing to do because your whole culture is based on condemnation, judgement and evaluation; you have been brought up on 'Do this and not that'. But if you can look in the mirror of relationship without creating the opposite, then you will find that there is no end to self-knowledge.

You see, the enquiry into self-knowledge is an outward movement which later turns inward; first we look at the stars, and then we look within ourselves. In the same way, we look for reality, for God, for security, happiness, in the objective world, and when it is not found there, we turn inward. This search for the inner God, the higher self, or what you will, completely ceases through self-knowledge, and then the mind becomes very quiet, not through discipline, but just through understanding, through watching, through being aware of itself every minute without choice. Don't say, 'I must be aware every minute', because that is just another manifestation of our foolishness when we want to get somewhere, when we want to arrive at a particular state. What matters is to be aware of yourself and to keep on being aware without accumulating because the moment you accumulate, from that centre you judge. Self-knowledge is not a process of accumulation, it is a process of discovery from moment to moment in relationship.

The Collected Works of J. Krishnamurti: vol. VIII
Bombay, February 20, 1955

Question: *Will you please explain what you mean by awareness?*

KRISHNAMURTI: Just simple awareness! Awareness of your judgements, your prejudices, your likes and dislikes. When you see something, that seeing is the outcome of your comparison, condemnation, judgement, evaluation, is it not? When you read something, you are judging, you are criticizing, you are condemning or approving. To be aware is to see, in the very moment, this whole process of judging, evaluating, the conclusions, the conformity, the acceptances, the denials.

Now, can one be aware without all that? At present all we know is a process of evaluating, and that evaluation is the outcome of our conditioning, of our background, of our religious, moral and educational influences. Such so-called awareness is the result of our memory — memory as the 'me', the Dutchman, the Hindu, the Buddhist, the Catholic, or whatever it may be. It is the 'me' — my memories, my family, my property, my qualities — which is looking, judging, evaluating. With that we are quite familiar, if we are at all alert. Now, can there be awareness without all that, without the self? Is it possible just to look without condemnation, just to observe the movement of the mind, one's own mind, without judging, without evaluating, without saying, 'It is good' or 'It is bad'?

The awareness which springs from the self, which is the awareness of evaluation and judgement, always creates duality, the conflict of the opposites — that 'which is' and that 'which should be'. In that awareness there is judgement, there is fear, there is evaluation, condemnation, identification. That is but the awareness of the 'me', of the self, of the 'I', with all its traditions, memories, and all the rest of it. Such awareness always creates conflict between the observer and the observed, between what I am and what I should be. Now, is it possible to be aware without this process of condemnation, judgement, evaluation? Is it possible to look at myself, whatever my thoughts are, and not condemn, not judge, not evaluate? I do not know if you have ever tried it. It is quite arduous because all our training from childhood leads us to condemn or to approve. And in the process of condemnation and approval, there is frustration, there is fear, there is a gnawing pain, anxiety, which is the very process of the 'me', the self.

So, knowing all that, can the mind, without effort, without trying not to condemn — because the moment it says, 'I mustn't condemn', it is already caught in the process of condemnation — can the mind be aware without judgement?

Can it just watch, with dispassion, and so observe the very thoughts and feelings themselves in the mirror of relationship — relationship with things, with people, and with ideas? Such silent observation does not breed aloofness, an icy intellectualism — on the contrary. If I would understand something, obviously there must be no condemnation, there must be no comparison — surely, that is simple. But we think understanding comes through comparison, so we multiply comparisons. Our education is comparative, and our whole moral, religious structure is to compare and condemn.

So the awareness of which I am speaking is the awareness of the whole process of condemnation, and the ending of it. In that there is observation without any judgement — which is extremely difficult; it implies the cessation, the ending of all terming, naming. When I am aware that I am greedy, acquisitive, angry, passionate, or what you will, is it not possible just to observe it, to be aware of it, without condemning? — which means putting an end to the very naming of the feeling. For when I give a name, such as 'greed', that very naming is the process of condemning. To us, neurologically, the very word 'greed' is already a condemnation. To free the mind from all condemnation means putting an end to all naming. After all, the naming is the process of the thinker. It is the thinker separating himself from thought — which is a totally artificial process — it is unreal. There is only thinking; there is no thinker; there is only a state of experiencing, not the entity who experiences.

So this whole process of awareness, observation, is the process of meditation. It is, if I can put it differently, the willingness to invite thought. For most of us, thoughts come in without invitation — one thought after another; there is no end to thinking; the mind is a slave to every kind of vagrant thought. If you realize that, then you will see that there can be an invitation to thought — an inviting of thought and then a pursuing of every thought that arises. For most of us, thought comes uninvited; it comes any old way. To understand that process, and then to invite thought and pursue that thought through to the end, is the whole process which I have described as awareness; and in that there is no naming. Then you will see that the mind becomes extraordinarily quiet — not through fatigue, not through discipline, not through any form of self-torture and control. Through awareness of its own activities, the mind becomes astonishingly quiet, still, creative — without the action of any discipline or any enforcement.

Then in that stillness of mind comes that which is true, without invitation. You cannot invite truth; it is the unknown. And in that silence there is no experiencer. Therefore that which is experienced is not stored, is not remembered as 'my experience of truth'. Then something which is timeless comes into being — that which cannot be measured by the one who has experienced, or who merely remembers a past experience. Truth is something which comes from moment to moment. It is not to be cultivated, not to be gathered, stored up and held in memory. It comes only when there is an awareness in which there is no experiencer.

The Collected Works of J. Krishnamurti: vol. IX
Amsterdam, May 26, 1955

Question: *Listening to you, one feels that you have read a great deal and are also directly aware of reality. If this is so, then why do you condemn the acquisition of knowledge?*

KRISHNAMURTI: I will tell you why. It is a journey that must be taken alone, and there can be no journeying alone if your companion is knowledge. If you have read the Gita, the Upanishads, and modern psychology, if you have gathered information about yourself from the experts, and about what they say you should strive after — such knowledge is an impediment. The treasure is not in books but buried in your own mind, and the mind alone can discover this treasure. To have self-knowledge is to know the ways of your mind, to be aware of its subtleties with all their implications, and for that you don't have to read a single book. As a matter of fact, I have not read any of these things. Perhaps as a boy, or a young man, I casually looked at some of the sacred books, but I have never studied them. I do not want to study them; they are tiresome because the treasure is somewhere else. The treasure is not in the books, nor in your guru; it is in yourself, and the key to it is the understanding of your own mind. You must understand your mind, not according to Patanjali, or according to some psychologist who is clever at explaining things, but by watching yourself, by observing how your mind works, not only the conscious mind, but the deep layers of the unconscious as well. If you watch your mind, play with it, look at it when it is spontaneous, free, it will reveal to you untold treasures; and then you are beyond all the books. But that again requires a great deal of attention, vigour, an intensity of pursuit — not the dilettantism of lazy explanations. So the mind must be free from knowledge because a mind that is occupied with knowledge can never discover 'what is'.

The Collected Works of J. Krishnamurti: vol. IX
Bombay, March 25, 1956

III

Writings

Problems and Escapes

'I have many serious problems and I seem to make them more tortuous and painful by trying to solve them. I am at my wit's end and I do not know what to do. Added to all this, I am deaf and have to use this beastly thing as an aid to my hearing. I have several children, and a husband who has left me. I am really concerned over my children, as I want them to avoid all the miseries I have been through.'

How anxious we are to find an answer to our problems! We are so eager to find an answer that we cannot study the problem; it prevents our silent observation of the problem. The problem is the important thing, and not the answer. If we look for an answer, we will find it; but the problem will persist, for the answer is irrelevant to the problem. Our search is for an escape from the problem, and the solution is a superficial remedy, so there is no understanding of the problem. All problems arise from one source, and without understanding the source, any attempt to solve the problems will only lead to further confusion and misery. One must first be very clear that one's intention to understand the problem is serious, that one sees the necessity of being free of all problems; for only then can the maker of problems be approached. Without freedom from problems, there can be no tranquillity; and tranquillity is essential for happiness, which is not an end in itself. As the pool is still when the breezes stop, so the mind is still with the cessation of problems. But the mind cannot be made still; if it is, it is dead, it is a stagnant pool. When this is clear, then the maker of the problems can be observed. The observation must be silent and not according to any predetermined plan based on pleasure and pain.

'But you are asking the impossible! Our education trains the mind to distinguish, to compare, to judge, to choose, and it is very difficult not to condemn or justify what is observed. How can one be free of this conditioning and observe silently?'

If you see that silent observation, passive awareness is essential for understanding, then the truth of your perception liberates you from the background. It is only when you do not see the immediate necessity of passive and yet alert awareness that the 'how', the search for a means to dissolve the background, arises. It is truth that liberates, not the means or the system. The truth that silent observation alone brings understanding must be seen; then only are you free from condemnation and justification. When you see danger, you do not ask how you are to keep away from it. It is because you do not see the necessity of being passively aware that you ask 'how'. Why do you not see the necessity of it?

'I want to, but I have never thought along these lines before. All I can say is that I want to get rid of my problems, because they are a real torture to me. I want to be happy, like any other person.'

Consciously or unconsciously we refuse to see the essentiality of being passively aware because we do not really want to let go of our problems; for what would we be without them? We would rather cling to something we know, however painful, than risk the pursuit of something that may lead who knows where. With the problems, at least, we are familiar; but the thought of pursuing the maker of them, not knowing where it may lead, creates in us fear and dullness. The mind would be lost without the worry of problems; it feeds on problems, whether they are world or kitchen problems, political or personal, religious or ideological; so our problems make us petty and narrow. A mind that is consumed with world problems is as petty as the mind that worries about the spiritual progress it is making. Problems burden the mind with fear, for problems give strength to the self, to the 'me' and the 'mine'. Without problems, without achievements and failures, the self is not.

'But without the self, how can one exist at all? It is the source of all action.'

As long as action is the outcome of desire, of memory, of fear, of pleasure and pain, it must inevitably breed conflict, confusion and antagonism. Our action is the outcome of our conditioning, at whatever level; and our response to challenge, being inadequate and incomplete, must produce conflict, which is the problem. Conflict is the very structure of the self. It is entirely possible to live without conflict, the conflict of greed, of fear, of success; but this possibility will be merely theoretical and not actual until it is discovered through direct experiencing. To exist without greed is possible only when the ways of the self are understood.

'Do you think my deafness is due to my fears and repressions? Doctors have assured me that there is nothing structurally wrong, and is there any possibility of recovering my hearing? I have been suppressed, in one way or another, all my life; I have never done anything that I really wanted to do.'

Inwardly and outwardly it is easier to repress than to understand. To understand is arduous, especially for those who have been heavily conditioned from childhood. Although strenuous, repression becomes a matter of habit. Understanding can never be made into a habit, a matter of routine; it demands constant watchfulness, alertness. To understand, there must be pliability, sensitivity, a warmth that has nothing to do with sentimentality. Suppression in any form needs no quickening of awareness; it is the easiest and the stupidest way to deal with responses. Suppression is conformity to an idea, to a pattern, and it offers superficial security, respectability. Understanding is liberating, but suppression is always narrowing, self-enclosing. Fear of authority, of insecurity, of opinion, builds up an ideological refuge, with its physical counterpart, to which the mind turns. This refuge, at whatever level it may be placed, ever sustains fear; and from fear there is substitution, sublimation or discipline, which are all a form of repression. Repression must find an outlet, which may be a physical ailment or some kind of ideological illusion. The price is paid according to one's temperament and idiosyncrasies.

'I have noticed that whenever there is something unpleasant to be heard, I take refuge behind this instrument, which thereby helps me to escape into my own world. But how is one to be free from the repression of years? Will it not take a long time?'

It is not a question of time, of dredging into the past, or of careful analysis; it is a matter of seeing the truth of repression. By being passively aware, without any choice, of the whole process of repression, the truth of it is immediately seen. The truth of repression cannot be discovered if we think in terms of yesterday and tomorrow; truth is not to be comprehended through the passage of time. Truth is not a thing to be attained; it is seen or it is not seen, it cannot be perceived gradually. The will to be free from repression is a hindrance to understanding the truth of it; for will is desire, whether positive or negative, and with desire there can be no passive awareness. It is desire or craving that brought about the repression; and this same desire, though now called will, can never free itself from its own creation. Again, the truth of will must be perceived through passive yet alert awareness. The analyser, though he may separate himself from it, is part of the analysed; and as he is conditioned by the thing he analyses, he cannot free himself from it. Again, the truth of this must be seen. It is truth that liberates, not will and effort.

Commentaries on Living

Obsession

He said he was obsessed by stupid little things, and that these obsessions constantly changed. He would worry over some imaginary physical defect, and within a few hours his worry would have fixed itself upon another incident or thought. He seemed to live from one anxious obsession to another. To overcome these obsessions, he continued, he would consult books or talk over his problems with a friend, and he had also been to a psychologist; but somehow he had found no relief. Even after a serious and absorbing meeting, these obsessions would immediately come on. If he found the cause, would it put an end to them?

Does discovery of a cause bring freedom from the effect? Will knowledge of the cause destroy the result? We know the causes, both economic and psychological, of war, yet we encourage barbarity and self-destruction. After all, our motive in searching for the cause is the desire to be rid of the effect. This desire is another form of resistance or condemnation; and when there is condemnation, there is no understanding.

'Then what is one to do?' he asked.

Why is the mind dominated by these trivial and stupid obsessions? To ask 'why' is not to search for the cause as something apart from yourself which you have to find; it is merely to uncover the ways of your own thinking. So why is the mind occupied in this manner? Is it not because it is superficial, shallow, petty and therefore concerned with its own attractions?

'Yes,' he replied, 'that appears to be true; but not entirely, for I am a serious person.'

Apart from these obsessions, what is your thought occupied with?

'With my profession,' he said. 'I have a responsible position. The whole day and sometimes far into the night, my thoughts are taken up with my business. I read occasionally, but most of my time is spent with my profession.'

Do you like what you are doing?

'Yes, but it is not completely satisfactory. All my life I have been dissatisfied with what I am doing, but I cannot give up my present position, for I have certain obligations — and besides, I am getting on in years. What bothers me are these obsessions, and my increasing resentment towards my work as well as towards people. I have not been kind; I feel increasing anxiety about the future, and I never seem to have any peace. I do my work well, but . . .'

Why are you struggling against 'what is'? The house in which I live may be noisy, dirty, the furniture may be hideous, and there may be an utter lack of beauty about the whole thing; but for various reasons I may have to live there, I cannot go away to another house. It is then not a question of acceptance, but of seeing the obvious fact. If I do not see 'what is', I shall worry myself sick about that vase, about that chair or that picture; they will become my obsessions, and there will be resentment against people, against my work, and so on. If I could leave the whole thing and start over again, it would be a different matter; but I cannot. It is no good my rebelling against 'what is', the actual. The recognition of 'what is' does not lead to smug contentment and ease. When I yield to 'what is', there is not only the understanding of it, but there also comes a certain quietness to the surface mind. If the surface mind is not quiet, it indulges in obsessions, actual or imaginary; it gets caught up in some social reform or religious conclusion; the Master, the saviour, the ritual, and so on. It is only when the surface mind is quiet that the hidden can reveal itself. The hidden must be exposed; but this is not possible if the surface mind is burdened with obsessions, worries. Since the surface mind is constantly in some kind of agitation, conflict is inevitable between the upper and the deeper levels of the mind; and as long as this conflict is not resolved, obsessions increase. After all, obsessions are a means of escape from our conflict. All escapes are similar, though it is obvious that some are socially more harmful.

When one is aware of the total process of obsession or of any other problem, only then is there freedom from the problem. To be extensively aware, there must be no condemnation or justification of the problem; awareness must be choiceless. To be so aware demands wide patience and sensitivity, it requires eagerness and sustained attention so that the whole process of thinking can be observed and understood.

Commentaries on Living

Why is There this Sorrow of Death?

Meditation is the unfolding of the new. The new is beyond and above the repetitious past — and meditation is the ending of this repetition. The death that meditation brings about is the immortality of the new. The new is not within the area of thought, and meditation is the silence of thought.

Meditation is not an achievement, nor is it the capture of a vision, nor the excitement of sensation. It is like the river, not to be tamed, swiftly running and overflowing its banks. It is the music without sound; it cannot be domesticated and made use of. It is the silence in which the observer has ceased from the very beginning.

The sun wasn't up yet; you could see the morning star through the trees. There was a silence that was really extraordinary. Not the silence between two noises or between two notes, but the silence that has no reason whatsoever — the silence that must have been at the beginning of the world. It filled the whole valley and the hills. The two big owls, calling to each other, never disturbed that silence, and a distant dog barking at the late moon was part of this immensity. The dew was especially heavy, and as the sun came up over the hill it was sparkling with many colours and with the glow that comes with the sun's first rays.

The delicate leaves of the jacaranda were heavy with dew, and birds came to have their morning baths, fluttering their wings so that the dew on those delicate leaves filled their feathers. The crows were particularly persistent; they would hop from one branch to another, pushing their heads through the leaves, fluttering their wings and preening themselves. There were about half-a-dozen of them on that one heavy branch, and there were many other birds, scattered all over the tree, taking their morning bath.

And this silence spread, and seemed to go beyond the hills. There were the usual noises of children shouting, and laughter; and the farm began to wake up.

It was going to be a cool day, and now the hills were taking on the light of the sun. They were very old hills — probably the oldest in the world — with oddly shaped rocks that seemed to be carved out with great care, balanced one on top of the other; but no wind or touch could loosen them from this balance.

It was a valley far removed from towns, and the road through it led to another village. The road was rough and there were no cars or buses to disturb the ancient quietness of this valley. There were bullock carts, but their movement was a part of the hills. There was a dry river-bed that only flowed with water after heavy rains, and the colour was a mixture of red, yellow and brown; and it, too, seemed to move with the hills. And the villagers who walked silently by were like the rocks.

The day wore on and towards the end of the evening, as the sun was setting over the western hills, the silence came in from afar, over the hills, through the trees, covering the little bushes and the ancient banyan. And as the stars became brilliant, so the silence grew into great intensity; you could hardly bear it.

The little lamps of the village were put out, and with sleep the intensity of that silence grew deeper, wider and incredibly overpowering. Even the hills became more quiet, for they, too, had stopped their whisperings, their movement, and seemed to lose their immense weight.

She said she was forty-five; she was carefully dressed in a sari, with some bangles on her wrists. The older man with her said he was her uncle. We all sat on the floor overlooking a big garden with a banyan tree, a few mango trees, the bright bougainvillea and the growing palms. She was terribly sad. Her hands were restless and she was trying to prevent herself from bursting into speech and perhaps tears. The uncle said: 'We have come to talk to you about my niece. Her husband died a few years ago, and then her son, and now she can't stop crying and has aged terribly. We don't know what to do. The usual doctors' advice doesn't seem to work, and she seems to be losing contact with her other children. She's getting thinner. We don't know where all this is going to end, and she insisted that we should come to see you.'

'I lost my husband four years ago. He was a doctor and died of cancer. He must have hidden it from me, and only in the last year or so did I know about it. He was in agony although the doctors gave him morphine and other sedatives. Before my eyes he withered away and was gone.'

She stopped, almost choking with tears. There was a dove sitting on a branch, quietly cooing. It was brownish-grey, with a small head and a large body — not too large, for it was a dove. Presently it flew off and the branch was swinging up and down from the pressure of its flight.

'I somehow cannot bear this loneliness, this meaningless existence without him. I loved my children; I had three of them, a boy and two girls. One day last year the boy wrote to me from school that he was not feeling well, and a few days later I got a telephone call from the headmaster, saying that he was dead.'

Here she began to sob uncontrollably. Presently she produced a letter from the boy in which he had said that he wanted to come home for he was not feeling well, and that he hoped she was all right. She explained that he had been concerned about her; he hadn't wanted to go to school but had wanted to remain with her. And she more or less forced him to go, afraid that he would be affected by her grief. Now it was too late. The two girls, she said, were not fully aware of all that had happened for they were quite young. Suddenly she burst out: 'I don't know what to do. This death has shaken the very foundations of my life. Like a house, our marriage was carefully built on what we considered a deep foundation. Now everything is destroyed by this enormous event.'

The uncle must have been a believer, a traditionalist, for he added: 'God has visited this on her. She has been through all the necessary ceremonies but they have not helped her. I believe in reincarnation, but she takes no comfort in it. She doesn't even want to talk about it. To her it is all meaningless and we have not been able to give her any comfort.'

We sat there in silence for some time. Her handkerchief was now quite wet; a clean handkerchief from the drawer helped to wipe away the tears on her cheeks. The red bougainvillea was peeping through the window, and the bright southern light was on every leaf.

Do you want to talk about this seriously — go to the root of it all? Or do you want to be comforted by some explanation, by some reasoned argument, and be distracted from your sorrow by some satisfying words?

She replied: 'I'd like to go into it deeply, but I don't know whether I have the capacity or the energy to face what you are going to say. When my husband was alive we used to come to some of your talks; but now I may find it very difficult to go along with you.'

Why are you in sorrow? Don't give an explanation, for that will only be a verbal construction of your feeling, which will not be the actual fact. So when we ask a question, please don't answer it. Just listen, and find out for yourself. Why is there this sorrow of death — in every house, rich and poor, from the most powerful in the land to the beggar? Why are you in sorrow? Is it for your husband — or is it for yourself? If you are crying for him, can your tears help him? He has gone irrevocably. Do what you will, you will never have him back. No tears, no belief, no ceremonies or gods can ever bring him back. It is a fact which you have to accept; you can't do anything about it. But if you are crying for yourself, because of your loneliness, your empty life, because of the sensual pleasures you had and the companionship, then you are crying, aren't you, out of your own emptiness and out of self-pity? Perhaps for the first time you are aware of your own inward poverty. You have invested in your husband, haven't you, if we may gently point it out, and it has given you comfort, satisfaction and pleasure? All you are feeling now — the sense of loss, the agony of loneliness and anxiety — is a form of self-pity, isn't it? Do look at it. Don't harden your heart against it and say: 'I love my husband, and I wasn't thinking a bit about myself. I wanted to protect him, even though I often tried to dominate him; but it was all for his sake and there was never a thought for myself.' Now that he has gone you are realizing, aren't you, your own actual state? His death has shaken you and shown you the actual state of your mind and heart. You may not be willing to look at it; you may reject it out of fear, but if you observe a little more you will see that you are crying out of your own loneliness, out of your inward poverty — which is out of self-pity.

'You are rather cruel, aren't you, sir?' she said. 'I have come to you for real comfort, and what are you giving me?'

It is one of the illusions most people have — that there is such a thing as inward comfort; that somebody else can give it to you or that you can find it for yourself. I am afraid there is no such thing. If you are seeking comfort you are bound to live in illusion, and when that illusion is broken you become sad because the comfort is taken away from you. So to understand sorrow or to go beyond it, one must see actually what is inwardly taking place, and not cover it up. To point out all this is not cruelty, is it? It's not something ugly from which to shy away. When you see all this, very clearly, then you come out of it immediately, without a scratch, unblemished, fresh, untouched by the events of life. Death is inevitable for all of us; one cannot escape from it. We try to find every kind of explanation, cling to every kind of belief in the hope of going beyond it, but do what you will it is always there; tomorrow, or round the corner, or many years away — it is always there. One has to come into touch with this enormous fact of life.

'But' said the uncle, and out came the traditional belief in Atman, the soul, the permanent entity which continues. He was on his own ground now, well-trodden with cunning arguments and quotations. You saw him suddenly sit up straight and the light of battle, the battle of words, came into his eyes. Sympathy, love and understanding were gone. He was on his sacred ground of belief, of tradition, trodden down by the heavy weight of conditioning. 'But the Atman is in every one of us! It is reborn and continues until it realizes that it is Brahman. We must go through sorrow to come to that reality. We live in illusion; the world is an illusion. There is only one reality.'

And he was off! She looked at me, not paying much attention to him, and a gentle smile began to appear on her face; and we both looked at the dove which had come back, and the bright red bougainvillea.

There is nothing permanent either on earth or in ourselves. Thought can give continuity to something it thinks about; it can give permanency to a word, to an idea, to a tradition. Thought thinks itself permanent, but is it permanent? Thought is the response of memory, and is that memory permanent? It can build an image and give to that image a continuity, a permanency, calling it Atman or whatever you like, and it can remember the face of the husband or the wife and hold on to it. All this is the activity of thought which creates fear, and out of this fear there is the drive for permanency — the fear of not having a meal tomorrow, or shelter — the fear of death. This fear is the result of thought, and Brahman is the product of thought, too.

The uncle said: 'Memory and thought are like a candle. You put it out and re-light it again; you forget, and you remember again later on. You die and are reborn again into another life. The flame of the candle is the same — and not the same. So in the flame there is a certain quality of continuity.'

But the flame which has been put out is not the same flame as the new. There is an ending of the old for the new to be. If there is a constant modified continuity, then there is no new thing at all. The thousand yesterdays cannot be made new; even a candle burns itself out. Everything must end for the new to be.

The uncle now cannot rely on quotations or beliefs or on the sayings of others, so he withdraws into himself and becomes quiet, puzzled and rather angry, for he has been exposed to himself, and, like his niece, doesn't want to face the fact.

'I am not concerned about all this,' she said. 'I am utterly miserable. I have lost my husband and my son, and there are these two children left. What am I to do?'

If you are concerned about the two children, you can't be concerned about yourself and your misery. You have to look after them, educate them rightly, bring them up without the usual mediocrity. But if you are consumed by your own self-pity, which you call 'the love for your husband', and if you withdraw into isolation, then you are also destroying the other two children. Consciously or unconsciously we are all utterly selfish, and so long as we get what we want we consider everything is all right. But the moment an event takes place to shatter all this, we cry out in despair, hoping to find other comforts which, of course, will again be shattered. So this process goes on, and if you want to be caught in it, knowing full well all the implications of it, then go ahead. But if you see the absurdity of it all, then you will naturally stop crying, stop isolating yourself, and live with the children with a new light and with a smile on your face.

The Only Revolution

Security

The small stream was flowing very gently beside the path that wound round the rice fields, and it was crowded with lotuses; they were dark violet with golden hearts, and they were clear of the water. Their scent remained close to them, and they were very beautiful. The sky was overcast; it was beginning to drizzle, and there was thunder among the clouds. The lightning was still far way, but it was coming towards the tree under which we were sheltering. It began to rain heavily, and the lotus leaves were collecting drops of water; when the drops became too large, they slipped off the leaves, only to form again. The lightning was now above the tree, and the cattle were frightened and straining at their ropes. A black calf, wet and shivering, was calling piteously; it broke its rope and ran towards a nearby hut. The lotuses were closing themselves tightly, shutting their hearts against the gathering darkness; one would have had to tear the violet petal to get at the golden hearts. They would remain tightly closed till the coming of the sun. Even in their sleep they were beautiful. The lightning was moving towards the town; it was now quite dark, and one could just hear the murmur of the stream. The path led past the village to the road which took us back to the noisy town.

He was a young man, in his twenties; he was well fed, had travelled a little and been to college. He was nervous and there was anxiety in his eyes. It was late, but he wanted to talk; he wanted someone to explore his mind for him. He exposed himself very simply, without any hesitation or pretension. His problem was clear, but not to him; he went groping about.

We do not listen and discover 'what is'; we foist our ideas and opinions on another, trying to force the other into the frame of our thought. Our own thoughts and judgements are so much more important to us than to find out 'what is'. The 'what is' is always simple; it is we who are complex. We make the simple, the 'what is', complex, and we get lost in it. We listen only to the increasing noise of our own confusion. To listen, we must be free. It is not that there must be no distractions, for thinking itself is a form of distraction. We must be free to be silent, and only then is it possible to hear.

He was saying that just as he was going off to sleep he would sit up with a start of naked fear. Then the room would lose its proportions; the walls would go flat, there would be no roof, and the floor would disappear. He would be frightened and sweating. This had been going on for many years.

What are you frightened of?

'I don't know; but when I wake up with fear, I go to my sister, or to my father and mother and talk with them for some time to calm myself, and then go off to sleep. They understand, but I am in my twenties and it is getting rather silly.'

Are you anxious about the future?

'Yes, somewhat. Though we have money, I am still rather anxious about it.'

Why?

'I want to marry and provide comfort for my future wife.'

Why be anxious about the future? You are quite young, and you can work and give her what is necessary. Why be so preoccupied with this? Are you afraid of losing your social position?

'Partly. We have a car, some property and reputation. Naturally I don't want to lose all this, which may be the cause of my fear. But it isn't quite this. It is the fear of not being. When I wake up with fear, I feel I am lost, that I am nobody, that I am falling to pieces.'

After all, a new government may come in and you may lose your property, your holdings; but you are quite young, and you can always work. Millions are losing their worldly goods, and you too may have to face that. Besides, the things of the world are to be shared and not to be exclusively possessed. At your age, why be so conservative, so afraid of losing?

'You see, I want to marry a particular girl, and I am anxious that nothing should stop it. Nothing is likely to stop it, but I miss her and she misses me, and this may be another cause of my fear.'

Is that the cause of your fear? You say that nothing out of the ordinary is likely to happen to prevent your marrying her, so why this fear?

'Yes, it is true that we can marry whenever we decide to, so that cannot be the cause of my fear, at least not now. I think I am really frightened of not being, of losing my identity, my name.'

Even if you did not care about your name but had your property and so on, would you not still be afraid? What do we mean by identity? It is to be identified with a name, with property, with a person, with ideas; it is to be associated with something, to be recognized as this or that, to be labelled as belonging to a particular group or country, and so on. You are afraid of losing your label, is that it?

'Yes. Otherwise, what am I? Yes, that is it.'

So you *are* your possessions. Your name and reputation, your car and other property, the girl you are going to marry, the ambitions that you have — you *are* these things. These things, together with certain characteristics and values, go to make up what you call 'I'; you are the sum total of all this, and you are afraid of losing it. As with everyone else, there is always the possibility of a loss; a war may come, there may be a revolution or a change in government towards the left. Something may happen to deprive you of these things, now or tomorrow. But why be afraid of insecurity? Is not insecurity the very nature of all things? Against this insecurity you are building walls that will protect you but these walls can be and are being broken down. You may escape from it for a time, but the danger of insecurity is always there. That which *is*, you cannot avoid; insecurity is there, whether you like it or not. This does not mean that you must resign yourself to it, or that you must accept or deny it; but you are young and why be afraid of insecurity?

'Now that you put it this way, I don't think I am afraid of insecurity. I really don't mind working; I work over eight hours a day at my job, and though I don't particularly like it, I can carry on. No, I am not afraid of losing property, the car, and so on; and my fiancee and I can marry whenever we want to. I see now that it is none of this that is making me fearful. Then what is it?'

Let us find out together. I might be able to tell you, but it would not be your discovery; it would only be on the verbal level, and so utterly useless. The finding of it will be your own experiencing of it, and it is this that is really important. Discovering is experiencing; we will discover it together.

If it is none of these things that you are frightened of losing, if you are not afraid of being insecure outwardly, then of what are you anxious? Don't answer right away, just listen, be watchful to find out. Are you quite sure it is not physical insecurity that you are frightened of? As far as one can be sure of such things, you say that you are not frightened of it. If you are sure that this is not a mere verbal assertion, then of what are you afraid?

'I am quite sure I am not frightened of being physically insecure; we can marry and have what we need. It is something more than the mere loss of things that I am afraid of. But what is it?'

We will find out, but let us consider it quietly. You really want to find out, don't you?

'Of course I do, especially now that we have gone as far as this. What is it that I am frightened of?'

To find out we must be quiet, watchful, but not pressing. If you are not frightened of physical insecurity, are you frightened of being inwardly insecure, of being unable to achieve the end which you have set for yourself? Don't answer, just listen. Do you feel incapable of becoming somebody? Probably you have a religious ideal; and do you feel you have not the capacity to live up to or achieve it? Do you feel a sense of hopelessness about it, a sense of guilt or frustration?

'You are perfectly right. Ever since I heard you some years ago as a boy, it has been my ideal, if I may say so, to be like you. It's in our blood to be religious, and I have felt I could be like that; but there has always been a deep fear of never coming near it.'

Let us go slowly. Though you are not frightened of being outwardly insecure, you are frightened of being insecure inwardly. Another man makes himself secure outwardly with a reputation, with fame, with money, and so on, while you want to be secure inwardly with an ideal; and you feel that you have no capacity to become that ideal. Why do you want to become or achieve an ideal? Isn't it only to be secure, to feel safe? This refuge you call an ideal; but actually you want to be safe, protected. Is that it?

'Now that you point it out, that is exactly it.'

You have discovered this now, have you not? But let us proceed further. You see the obvious shallowness of outward security; but do you also see the falseness of seeking inward security through becoming the ideal? The ideal is your refuge, instead of money. Do you really see this?

'Yes, I really do.'

Then be what you are. When you see the falseness of the ideal, it drops away from you. You are 'what is'. From there proceed to understand 'what is' — but not towards any particular end, for the end, the goal is always away from 'what is'. The 'what is' is yourself, not at any particular period or in any given mood, but yourself as you are from moment to moment. Do not condemn yourself or become resigned to what you see, but be watchful without interpreting the movement of 'what is'. This will be arduous, but there is delight in it. Only to the free is there happiness, and freedom comes with the truth of 'what is'.

Commentaries on Living

Anger

Even at that altitude the heat was penetrating. The windowpanes felt warm to the touch. The steady hum of the plane's motors was soothing, and many of the passengers were dozing. The earth was far below us, shimmering in the heat, an unending brown with an occasional patch of green. Presently we landed, and the heat became all but unbearable; it was literally painful, and even in the shade of a building the top of one's head felt as if it would burst. The summer was well along and the country was almost a desert. We took off again and the plane climbed, seeking the cool winds. Two new passengers sat in the opposite seats and they were talking loudly; it was impossible not to overhear them. They began quietly enough; but soon anger crept into their voices, the anger of familiarity and resentment. In their violence they seemed to have forgotten the rest of the passengers; they were so upset with each other that they alone existed, and none else.

Anger has that peculiar quality of isolation; like sorrow, it cuts one off, and for the time being, at least, all relationship comes to an end. Anger has the temporary strength and vitality of the isolated. There is a strange despair in anger; for isolation is despair. The anger of disappointment, of jealousy, of the urge to wound, gives a violent release whose pleasure is self-justification. We condemn others, and that very condemnation is a justification of ourselves. Without some kind of attitude, whether of self-righteousness or self-abasement, what are we? We use every means to bolster ourselves up; and anger, like hate, is one of the easiest ways. Simple anger, a sudden flare-up which is quickly forgotten, is one thing; but the anger that is deliberately built up, that has been brewed and that seeks to hurt and destroy, is quite another matter. Simple anger may have some physiological cause which can be seen and remedied; but the anger that is the outcome of a psychological cause is much more subtle and difficult to deal with. Most of us do not mind being angry, we find an excuse for it. Why should we not be angry when there is ill-treatment of another or of ourselves? So we become righteously angry. We never just say we are angry, and stop there; we go into elaborate explanations of its cause. We never just say that we are jealous or bitter, but justify or explain it. We ask how there can be love without jealousy, or say that someone else's actions have made us bitter, and so on.

It is the explanation, the verbalization, whether silent or spoken, that sustains anger, that gives it scope and depth. The explanation, silent or spoken, acts as a shield against the discovery of ourselves as we are. We want to be praised or flattered, we expect something; and when these things do not take place, we are disappointed, we become bitter or jealous. Then, violently or softly, we blame someone else; we say the other is responsible for our bitterness. You are of great significance because I depend upon you for happiness, for my position or prestige. Through you, I fulfil, so you are important to me; I must guard you, I must possess you. Through you, I escape from myself; and when I am thrown back upon myself, being fearful of my own state, I become angry. Anger takes many forms: disappointment, resentment, bitterness, jealousy, and so on.

The storing up of anger, which is resentment, requires the antidote of forgiveness; but the storing up of anger is far more significant than forgiveness. Forgiveness is unnecessary when there is no accumulation of anger. Forgiveness is essential if there is resentment; but to be free from flattery and from the sense of injury, without the hardness of indifference, makes for mercy, charity. Anger cannot be got rid of by the action of will, for will is part of violence. Will is the outcome of desire, the craving to be; and desire in its very nature is aggressive, dominant. To suppress anger by the exertion of will is to transfer anger to a different level, giving it a different name; but it is still part of violence. To be free from violence, which is not the cultivation of non-violence, there must be the understanding of desire. There is no spiritual substitute for desire; it cannot be suppressed or sublimated. There must be a silent and choiceless awareness of desire; and this passive awareness is the direct experiencing of desire without an experiencer giving it a name.

Commentaries on Living

Conditioning

He was very concerned with helping humanity, with doing good works, and was active in various social welfare organizations. He said he had literally never taken a long holiday, and that since his graduation from college he had worked constantly for the betterment of man. Of course he wasn't taking any money for the work he was doing. His work had always been very important to him, and he was greatly attached to what he did. He had become a first class social worker, and he loved it. But he had heard something in one of the talks about the various kinds of escape which condition the mind, and he wanted to talk things over.

'Do you think being a social worker is conditioning? Does it only bring about further conflict?'

Let us find out what we mean by conditioning. When are we aware that we are conditioned? Are we ever aware of it? Are you aware that you are conditioned, or are you only aware of conflict, of struggle at various levels of your being? Surely, we are aware, not of our conditioning, but only of conflict, of pain and pleasure.

'What do you mean by conflict?'

Every kind of conflict: the conflict between nations, between various social groups, between individuals, and the conflict within oneself. Is not conflict inevitable as long as there is no integration between the actor and his action, between challenge and response? Conflict is our problem, is it not? Not any one particular conflict, but all conflict: the struggle between ideas, beliefs, ideologies, between the opposites. If there were no conflict there would be no problems.

'Are you suggesting that we should all seek a life of isolation, of contemplation?'

Contemplation is arduous, it is one of the most difficult things to understand. Isolation, though each one is consciously or unconsciously seeking it in his own way, does not solve our problems; on the contrary, it increases them. We are trying to understand what are the factors of conditioning which bring further conflict. We are only aware of conflict, of pain and pleasure, and we are not aware of our conditioning. What makes for conditioning?

'Social or environmental influences: the society in which we were born, the culture in which we have been raised, economic and political pressures, and so on.'

That is so; but is that all? These influences are our own product, are they not? Society is the outcome of man's relationship with man, which is fairly obvious. This relationship is one of use, of need, of comfort, of gratification, and it creates influences, values that bind us. The binding is our conditioning. By our own thoughts and actions we are bound; but we are not aware that we are bound, we are only aware of the conflict of pleasure and pain. We never seem to go beyond this; and if we do, it is only into further conflict. We are not aware of our conditioning, and until we are, we can only produce further conflict and confusion.

'How is one to be aware of one's conditioning?'

It is possible only by understanding another process, the process of attachment. If we can understand why we are attached, then perhaps we can be aware of our conditioning.

'Isn't that rather a long way round to come to a direct question?'

Is it? Just try to be aware of your conditioning. You can only know it indirectly, in relation to something else. You cannot be aware of your conditioning as an abstraction, for then it is merely verbal, without much significance. We are only aware of conflict. Conflict exists when there is no integration between challenge and response. This conflict is the result of our conditioning. Conditioning is attachment: attachment to work, to tradition, to property, to people, to ideas, and so on. If there were no attachment, would there be conditioning? Of course not. So why are we attached? I am attached to my country because through identification with it I become somebody. I identify myself with my work, and the work becomes important. I am my family, my property; I am attached to them. The object of attachment offers me the means of escape from my own emptiness. Attachment is escape, and it is escape that strengthens conditioning. If I am attached to you, it is because you have become the means of escape from myself; therefore you are very important to me and I must possess you, hold on to you. You become the conditioning factor, and escape is the conditioning. If we can be aware of our escapes, we can then perceive the factors, the influences that make for conditioning.

'Am I escaping from myself through social work?'

Are you attached to it, bound to it? Would you feel lost, empty, bored, if you did not do social work?

'I am sure I would.'

Attachment to your work is your escape. There are escapes at all the levels of our being. You escape through work, another through drink, another through religious ceremonies, another through knowledge, another through God, and still another is addicted to amusement. All escapes are the same, there is no superior or inferior escape. God and drink are on the same level as long as they are escapes from what we are. When we are aware of our escapes, only then can we know of our conditioning.

'What shall I do if I cease to escape through social work? Can I do anything without escaping? Is not all my action a form of escape from what I am?'

Is this question merely verbal, or does it reflect an actuality, a fact which you are experiencing? If you did not escape, what would happen? Have you ever tried it?

'What you are saying is so negative, if I may say so. You don't offer any substitute for work.'

Is not all substitution another form of escape? When one particular form of activity is not satisfactory or brings further conflict, we turn to another. To replace one activity by another without understanding escape is rather futile, is it not? It is these escapes and our attachment to them that make for conditioning. Conditioning brings problems, conflict. It is conditioning that prevents our understanding of the challenge; being conditioned, our response must inevitably create conflict.

'How can one be free from conditioning?'

Only by understanding, being aware of our escapes. Our attachment to a person, to work, to an ideology, is the conditioning factor; this is the thing we have to understand, and not seek a better or more intelligent escape. All escapes are unintelligent, as they inevitably bring about conflict. To cultivate detachment is another form of escape, of isolation; it is attachment to an abstraction, to an ideal called detachment. The ideal is fictitious, ego-made, and becoming the ideal is an escape from 'what is'. There is the understanding of 'what is', an adequate action towards 'what is', only when the mind is no longer seeking any escape. The very thinking about 'what is' is an escape from 'what is'.

Thinking about the problem is escape from the problem; for thinking is the problem, and the only problem. The mind, unwilling to be what it is, fearful of what it is, seeks these various escapes; and the way of escape is thought. As long as there is thinking, there must be escapes, attachments, which only strengthen conditioning.

Freedom from conditioning comes with the freedom from thinking. When the mind is utterly still, only then is there freedom for the real to be.

Commentaries on Living: Second Series

Self-esteem

She had come with three of her friends; they were all earnest and had the dignity of intelligence. One was quick to grasp, another was impatient in his quickness, and the third was eager, but the eagerness was not sustained. They made a good group, for they all shared the problem of their friend, and no one offered advice or weighty opinions. They all wanted to help her do whatever she thought was the right thing, and not merely act according to tradition, public opinion or personal inclination. The difficulty was, what was the right thing to do? She herself was not sure, she felt disturbed and confused. But there was much pressure for immediate action; a decision had to be made, and she could not postpone it any longer. It was a question of freedom from a particular relationship. She wanted to be free, and she repeated this several times.

There was quietness in the room; the nervous agitation had subsided, and they were all eager to go into the problem without expecting a result, a definition of the right thing to do. The right action would emerge, naturally and fully, as the problem was exposed. The discovery of the content of the problem was important, and not the end-result; for any answer would only be another conclusion, another opinion, another piece of advice, which would in no way solve the problem. The problem itself had to be understood, and not how to respond to the problem or what to do about it. The right approach to the problem was important, because the problem itself held the right action.

The waters of the river were dancing, for the sun had made on them a path of light. A white sail crossed the path, but the dance was not disturbed. It was a dance of pure delight. The trees were full of birds, scolding, preening, flying away only to come back again. Several monkeys were tearing off the tender leaves and stuffing them in their mouths; their weight bent the delicate branches into long curves, yet they held on lightly and were unafraid. With what ease they moved from branch to branch; though they jumped, it was a flow, the taking off and the landing were one movement. They would sit with their tails hanging and reach for the leaves. They were high up, and took no notice of the people passing below. As darkness approached, the parrots came by the hundred to settle down for the night among the thick leaves. One saw them come and disappear into the foliage. The new moon was just visible. Far away a train whistled as it was crossing the long bridge around the curve of the river. This river was sacred, and people came from far distances to bathe in it, that their sins might be washed away. Every river is lovely and sacred, and the beauty of this one was its wide, sweeping curve and the islands of sand between deep stretches of water; and those silent white sails that went up and down the river every day.

'I want to be free from a particular relationship,' she said.

What do you mean by wanting to be free? When you say, 'I want to be free', you imply that you are not free. In what way are you not free?

'I am free physically; I am free to come and go, because physically I am no longer the wife. But I want to be completely free; I do not want to have anything to do with that particular person.'

In what way are you related to that person, if you are already physically free? Are you related to him in any other way?

'I do not know, but I have great resentment against him. I do not want to have anything to do with him.'

You want to be free, and yet you have resentment against him? Then you are not free of him. Why have you this resentment against him?

'I have recently discovered what he is: his meanness, his real lack of love, his complete selfishness. I cannot tell you what a horror I have discovered in him. To think that I was jealous of him, that I idolized him, that I submitted to him! Finding him to be stupid and cunning when I thought him an ideal husband, loving and kind, has made me resentful of him. To think I had anything to do with him makes me feel unclean. I want to be completely free from him.'

You may be physically free from him, but as long as you have resentment against him, you are not free. If you hate him, you are tied to him; if you are ashamed of him, you are still enslaved by him. Are you angry with him, or with yourself? He is what he is, and why be angry with him? Is your resentment really against him? Or having seen 'what is', are you ashamed of yourself for having been associated with it? Surely, you are resentful, not of him, but of your own judgement, of your own actions. You are ashamed of yourself. Being unwilling to see this, you blame him for what he is. When you realize that your resentment against him is an escape from your own romantic idolization, then he is out of the picture. You are not ashamed of him, but of yourself for being associated with him. It is with yourself that you are angry, and not with him.

'Yes, that is so.'

If you really see this, experience it as fact, then you are free of him. He is no longer the object of your enmity. Hate binds as love does.

'But how am I to be free from my own shame, from my own stupidity? I see very clearly that he is what he is, and is not to be blamed; but how am I to be free of this shame, this resentment which has been slowly ripening in me and has come to fullness in this crisis? How am I to wipe out the past?'

Why you desire to wipe out the past is of more significance than knowing how to wipe it out. The intention with which you approach the problem is more important than knowing what to do about it. Why do you want to wipe out the memory of that association?

'I dislike the memory of all those years. It has left a very bad taste in my mouth. Is that not a good enough reason?'

Not quite, is it? Why do you want to wipe out those past memories? Surely, not because they leave a bad taste in your mouth. Even if you were able through some means to wipe out the past, you might again be caught in actions that you would be ashamed of. Merely wiping out the unpleasant memories does not solve the problem, does it?

'I thought it did; but what is the problem then? Are you not making it unnecessarily complex? It is already complex enough, at least my life is. Why add another burden to it?'

Are we adding a further burden, or are we trying to understand 'what is' and be free of it? Please have a little patience. What is the urge that is prompting you to wipe out the past? It may be unpleasant, but why do you want to wipe it out? You have a certain idea or picture of yourself which these memories contradict, and so you want to get rid of them. You have a certain estimation of yourself, have you not?

'Of course, otherwise . . .'

We all place ourselves at various levels, and we are constantly falling from these heights. It is the falls we are ashamed of. Self-esteem is the cause of our shame, of our fall. It is this self-esteem that must be understood, and not the fall. If there is no pedestal on which you have put yourself, how can there be any fall? Why have you put yourself on a pedestal called self-esteem, human dignity, the ideal, and so on? If you can understand this, then there will be no shame of the past; it will have completely gone. You will be what you are without the pedestal. If the pedestal is not there, the height that makes you look down or look up, then you are what you have always avoided. It is this avoidance of 'what is', of what you are, that brings about confusion and antagonism, shame and resentment. You do not have to tell me or another what you are, but be aware of what you are, whatever it is, pleasant or unpleasant: live with it without justifying or resisting it. Live with it without naming it; for the very term is a condemnation or an identification. Live with it without fear, for fear prevents communion, and without communion you cannot live with it. To be in communion is to love. Without love, you cannot wipe out the past; with love, there is no past. Love, and time is not.

Commentaries on Living

The Storm in the Mind

All day the fog had lasted, and as it cleared towards evening a wind sprang up from the east — a dry, harsh wind, blowing down the dead leaves and drying up the land. It was a tempestuous and menacing night; the wind had increased, the house creaked, and branches were being torn from the trees. The next morning the air was so clear you could almost touch the mountains. The heat had returned with the wind; but as the wind died in the late afternoon, the fog rolled in again from the sea.

How extraordinarily beautiful and rich the earth is! There is no tiring of it. The dry river-beds are full of living things: gorse, poppies, tall yellow sunflowers. On the boulders there are lizards; a brown-and white-ringed king snake is sunning itself, its black tongue shooting in and out, and across the ravine a dog is barking, pursuing a gopher or a rabbit.

Contentment is never the outcome of fulfilment, of achievement, or of the possession of things; it is not born of action or inaction. It comes with the fullness of 'what is', not in the alteration of it. That which is full does not need alteration, change. It is the incomplete which is trying to become complete that knows the turmoil of discontent and change. The 'what is' is the incomplete, it is not the complete. The complete is unreal, and the pursuit of the unreal is the pain of discontent which can never be healed. The very attempt to heal that pain is the search for the unreal, from which arises discontent. There is no way out of discontent. To be aware of discontent is to be aware of 'what is', and in the fullness of it there is a state which may be called contentment. It has no opposite.

The house overlooked the valley, and the highest peak of the distant mountains was aglow with the setting sun. Its rocky mass seemed hung from the sky and alight from within, and in the darkening room the beauty of that light was beyond all measure.

He was a youngish man, eager and searching.

'I have read several books on religion and religious practices, on meditation and the various methods advocated for attaining the highest. I was at one time drawn to Communism, but soon found that it was a retrogressive movement in spite of the many intellectuals who belonged to it. I was also attracted to Catholicism. Some of its doctrines pleased me, and for a time I thought of becoming a Catholic; but one day, while talking to a very learned priest, I suddenly perceived how similar Catholicism was to the prison of Communism. During my wanderings as a sailor on a tramp-ship I went to India and spent nearly a year there, and I thought of becoming a monk; but that was too withdrawn from life and too idealistically unreal. I tried living alone in order to meditate, but that too came to an end. After all these years I still seem to be utterly incapable of controlling my thoughts, and this is what I want to talk about. Of course I have other problems, sex and so on, but if I were completely the master of my thoughts I could then manage to curb my burning desires and urges.'

Will the controlling of thought lead to the calming of desire, or merely to its suppression, which will in turn bring other and deeper problems?

'You are of course not advocating giving way to desire. Desire is the way of thought, and in my attempts to control thought I had hoped to subjugate my desires. Desires have either to be subjugated or sublimated, but even to sublimate them they must first be held in check. Most of the teachers insist that desires must be transcended, and they prescribe various methods to bring this about.'

Apart from what others have said, what do you think? Will mere control of desire resolve the many problems of desire? Will suppression or sublimation of desire bring about the understanding of it, or free you from it? Through some occupation, religious or otherwise, the mind can be disciplined every hour of the day. But an occupied mind is not a free mind, and surely it is only the free mind that can be aware of timeless creativity.

'Is there no freedom in transcending desire?'

What do you mean by transcending desire?

'For the realization of one's own happiness, and also of the highest, it is necessary not to be driven by desire, not to be caught in its turmoil and confusion. To have desire under control, some form of subjugation is essential. Instead of pursuing the trivial things of life, that very same desire can search out the sublime.'

You may change the object of desire from a house to knowledge, from the low to the very highest, but it is still the activity of desire, is it not? One may not want worldly recognition, but the urge to attain heaven is still the pursuit of gain. Desire is ever seeking fulfilment, attainment, and it is this movement of desire which must be understood and not driven away or under. Without understanding the ways of desire, mere control of thought has little significance.

'But I must come back to the point from which I started. Even to understand desire, concentration is necessary, and that is my whole difficulty. I can't seem to control my thoughts. They wander all over the place, tumbling over each other. There is not a single thought that is dominant and continuous among all the irrelevant thoughts.'

The mind is like a machine that is working night and day, chattering, everlastingly busy whether asleep or awake. It is speedy and as restless as the sea. Another part of this intricate and complex mechanism tries to control the whole movement, and so begins the conflict between opposing desires, urges. One may be called the higher self and the other the lower self, but both are within the area of the mind. The action and reaction of the mind, of thought, are almost simultaneous and almost automatic. This whole conscious and unconscious process of accepting and denying, conforming and striving to be free, is extremely rapid. So the question is not how to control this complex mechanism, for control brings friction and only dissipates energy, but can this very swift mind slow down?

'But how?'

If it may be pointed out, sir, the issue is not the 'how'. The 'how' merely produces a result, an end without much significance; and after it is gained, another search for another desirable end will begin, with its misery and conflict.

'Then what is one to do?'

You are not asking the right question, are you? You are not discovering for yourself the truth or falseness of the slowing down of the mind, but you are concerned with getting a result. Getting a result is comparatively easy, isn't it? Is it possible for the mind to slow down without putting on brakes?

'What do you mean by slowing down?'

When you are going very fast in a car, the nearby landscape is a blur; it is only at a walking speed that you can observe in detail the trees, the birds and the flowers. Self-knowledge comes with the slowing down of the mind, but that doesn't mean forcing the mind to be slow.

Compulsion only makes for resistance, and there must be no dissipation of energy in the slowing down of the mind. This is so, isn't it?

'I think I am beginning to see that the effort one makes to control thought is wasteful, but I don't understand what else is to be done.'

We haven't yet come to the question of action, have we? We are trying to see that it is important for the mind to slow down, we are not considering how to slow it down. Can the mind slow down? And when does this happen?

'I don't know, I have never thought of it before.'

Have you not noticed, sir, that while you are watching something the mind slows down? When you watch that car moving along the road down there, or look intently at any physical object, is not your mind functioning more slowly? Watching, observing, does slow down the mind. Looking at a picture, an image, an object, helps to quiet the mind, as does the repetition of a phrase; but then the object or the phrase becomes very important, and not the slowing down of the mind and what is discovered thereby.

'I am watching what you are explaining, and there is an awareness of the stillness of the mind.'

Do we ever really watch anything, or do we interpose between the observer and the observed a screen of various prejudices, values, judgements, comparisons, condemnations?

'It is almost impossible not to have this screen. I don't think I am capable of observing in an inviolate manner.'

If it may be suggested, don't block yourself by words or by a conclusion, positive or negative. Can there be observation without this screen? To put it differently, is there attention when the mind is occupied? It is only the unoccupied mind that can attend. The mind is slow, alert, when there is watchfulness, which is the attention of an unoccupied mind.

'I am beginning to experience what you are saying, sir.'

Let us examine it a little further. If there is no evaluation, no screen between the observer and the observed, is there then a separation, a division between them? Is not the observer the observed?

'I am afraid I don't follow.'

The diamond cannot be separated from its qualities, can it? The feeling of envy cannot be separated from the experiencer of that feeling, though an illusory division does exist which breeds conflict, and in this conflict the mind is caught. When this false separation disappears, there is a possibility of freedom, and only then is the mind still. It is only when the experiencer ceases that there is the creative movement of the real.

Commentaries on Living: Second Series

IV

Diaries, Dictations, Letters

A Feeling for All Living Things

There is a tree by the river and we have been watching it day after day for several weeks when the sun is about to rise. As the sun rises slowly over the horizon, over the trees, this particular tree becomes all of a sudden golden. All the leaves are bright with life and as you watch it as the hours pass by, that tree whose name does not matter — what matters is that beautiful tree — an extraordinary quality seems to spread all over the land, over the river. And as the sun rises a little higher, the leaves begin to flutter, to dance. And each hour seems to give to that tree a different quality. Before the sun rises, it has a sombre feeling, quiet, far away, full of dignity. And as the day begins, the leaves with the light on them dance and give it that peculiar feeling that one has of great beauty. By midday its shadow has deepened and you can sit there protected from the sun, never feeling lonely, with the tree as your companion. As you sit there, there is a relationship of deep, abiding security and a freedom that only trees can know.

Towards the evening when the western skies are lit up by the setting sun, the tree gradually becomes sombre, dark, closing in on itself. The sky has become red, yellow, green, but the tree remains quiet, hidden, and is resting for the night.

If you establish a relationship with it, then you have relationship with mankind. You are responsible then for that tree and for the trees of the world. But if you have no relationship with the living things on this earth, you may lose whatever relationship you have with humanity, with human beings. We never look deeply into the quality of a tree; we never really touch it, feel its solidity, its rough bark, and hear the sound that is part of the tree. Not the sound of wind through the leaves, not the breeze of a morning that flutters the leaves, but its own sound, the sound of the trunk and the silent sound of the roots. You must be extraordinarily sensitive to hear the sound. This sound is not the noise of the world, not the noise of the chattering of the mind, not the vulgarity of human quarrels and human warfare but sound as part of the universe.

It is odd that we have so little relationship with nature, with the insects and the leaping frog, and the owl that hoots among the hills calling for its mate. We never seem to have a feeling for all living things on the earth. If we could establish a deep, abiding relationship with nature, we would never kill an animal for our appetite, we would never harm, vivisect a monkey, a dog, a guinea pig for our benefit. We would find other ways to heal our wounds, heal our bodies. But the healing of the mind is something totally different. That healing gradually takes place if you are with nature, with that orange on the tree, and the blade of grass that pushes through the cement, and the hills covered, hidden, by the clouds.

This is not sentiment or romantic imagination but a reality of a relationship with everything that lives and moves on the earth. Man has killed millions of whales and is still killing them. All that we derive from their slaughter can be had through other means. But apparently man loves to kill things, the fleeting deer, the marvellous gazelle, and the great elephant. We love to kill each other. This killing of other human beings has never stopped throughout the history of man's life on this earth. If we could, and we must, establish a deep, long, abiding relationship with nature, with the actual trees, the bushes, the flowers, the grass and the fast-moving clouds, then we would never slaughter another human being for any reason whatsoever. Organized murder is war, and though we demonstrate against a particular war, the nuclear, or any other kind of war, we have never demonstrated against war. We have never said that to kill another human being is the greatest sin on earth.

Krishnamurti to Himself

What is the Future of Mankind?

At the bird-feeder there were a dozen or more birds chirping away, pecking at the grains, struggling, fighting each other, and when another big bird came they all fluttered away. When the big bird left again, they all came back, chattering, quarrelling, chirping, making quite a lot of noise. Presently a cat went by and there was a flurry, a screeching and a great to-do. The cat was chased away — it was one of those wild cats, not a pet cat; there are a great many of those wild ones around here of different sizes, shapes and colours. At the feeder all day long there were birds, little ones and big ones, and then a blue-jay came scolding everybody, the whole universe, and chased the other birds away — or rather they left when it came. They were very watchful for cats. And as the evening drew close all the birds went away and there was silence, quiet, peaceful. The cats came and went, but there were no birds.

That morning the clouds were full of light and there was promise in the air of more rain. For the past few weeks it had been raining. There is an artificial lake and the waters were right to the top. All the green leaves and the shrubs and the tall trees were waiting for the sun, which hadn't appeared bright as the Californian sun is; it had not shown its face for many a day.

One wonders what is the future of mankind, the future of all those children you see shouting, playing — such happy, gentle, nice faces — what is their future? The future is what we are now. This has been so historically for many thousands of years — the living and dying, and all the travail of our lives. We don't seem to pay much attention to the future.

You see on television endless entertainment from morning until late in the night, except for one or two channels, but they are very brief and not too serious. The children are entertained. The commercials all sustain the feeling that you are being entertained. And this is happening practically all over the world. What will be the future of these children? There is the entertainment of sport — thirty, forty thousand people watching a few people in the arena and shouting themselves hoarse. And you also go and watch some ceremony being performed in a great cathedral, some ritual, and that too is a form of entertainment, only you call that holy, religious, but it is still an entertainment — a sentimental, romantic experience, a sensation of religiosity. Watching all this in different parts of the world, watching the mind being occupied with amusement, entertainment, sport, one must inevitably ask, if one is in any way concerned: What is the future? More of the same in different forms? A variety of amusements?

So you have to consider, if you are at all aware of what is happening to you, how the worlds of entertainment and sport are capturing your mind, shaping your life. Where is all this leading to? Or perhaps you are not concerned at all? You probably don't care about tomorrow. Probably you haven't given it thought, or, if you have, you may say it is too complex, too frightening, too dangerous to think of the coming years — not of your particular old age but of the destiny, if we can use that word, the result of our present way of life, filled with all kinds of romantic, emotional, sentimental feelings and pursuits, and the whole world of entertainment impinging on your mind. If you are at all aware of all this, what is the future of mankind?

As we said earlier, the future is what you are now. If there is no change — not superficial adaptations, superficial adjustments to any pattern, political, religious or social, but the change that is far deeper, demanding your attention, your care, your affection — if there is not a fundamental change, then the future is what we are doing every day of our life in the present. Change is rather a difficult word. Change to what? Change to another pattern? To another concept? To another political or religious system? Change from this to that? That is still within the realm, or within the field of 'what is'. Change to that is projected by thought, formulated by thought, materialistically determined.

So one must enquire carefully into this word 'change'. Is there a change if there is a motive? Is there a change if there is a particular direction, a particular end, a conclusion that seems sane, rational? Or perhaps a better phrase is 'the ending of what is'. The ending, not the movement of 'what is' to 'what should be'. That is not change. But the ending, the cessation, the — what is the right word? — I think 'ending' is a good word, so let's stick to that. The ending. But if the ending has a motive, a purpose, is a matter of decision, then it is merely a change from this to that. The word 'decision' implies the action of will. 'I will do this'; 'I won't do that'. When desire enters into the act of the ending, that desire becomes the cause of ending. Where there is a cause, there is a motive and so there is no real ending at all.

The twentieth century has had a tremendous lot of changes produced by two devastating wars, and the dialectical materialism, and the scepticism of religious beliefs, activities and rituals and so on, apart from the technological world which has brought about a great many changes; and there will be further changes when the computer is fully developed — you are just at the beginning of it. Then, when the computer takes over, what is going to happen to our human minds? That is a different question which we should go into another time.

When the industry of entertainment takes over, as it is gradually doing now, when the young people, the students, the children, are constantly instigated to pleasure, to fancy, to romantic sensuality, the words 'restraint' and 'austerity' are pushed away, never even given a thought. The austerity of the monks, the sannyasis, who deny the world, who clothe their bodies with some kind of uniform or just a cloth — this denial of the material world is surely not austerity. You probably won't even listen to this, to what the implications of austerity are. When you have been brought up from childhood to amuse yourself and escape from yourself through entertainment, religious or otherwise, and when most of the psychologists say that you must express everything you feel and that any form of holding back or restraint is detrimental, leading to various forms of neuroticism, you naturally enter more and more into the world of sport, amusement, entertainment, all helping you to escape from yourself, from what you are.

The understanding of the nature of what you are, without any distortions, without any bias, without any reactions to what you discover you are, is the beginning of austerity. The watching, the awareness, of every thought, every feeling, not to restrain it, not to control it, but to watch it, like watching a bird in flight, without any of your own prejudices and distortions — that watching brings about an extraordinary sense of austerity that goes beyond all restraint, all the fooling around with oneself and all this idea of self-improvement, self-fulfilment. That is all rather childish. In this watching there is great freedom and in that freedom there is the sense of the dignity of austerity. But if you said all this to a modern group of students or children, they would probably look out of the window in boredom because this world is bent on its own pursuit of pleasure.

A large fawn-coloured squirrel came down the tree and went up to the feeder, nibbled at a few grains, sat there on top of it, looked around with its large beady eyes, its tail up, curved — a marvellous thing. It sat there for a moment or so, came down, went along the few rocks and then dashed to the tree and up, and disappeared.

It appears that man has always escaped from himself, from what he is, from where he is going, from what all this is about — the universe, our daily life, the dying and the beginning. It is strange that we never realize that however much we may escape from ourselves, however much we may wander away consciously, deliberately, or unconsciously, subtly, the conflict, the pleasure, the pain, the fear and so on are always there. They ultimately dominate. You may try to suppress them, you may try to put them away deliberately with an act of will but they surface again. And pleasure is one of the factors that predominate; it too has the same conflicts, the same pain, the same boredom. The weariness of pleasure and the fret is part of this turmoil of our life. You can't escape it, my friend. You can't escape from this deep, unfathomed turmoil unless you really give thought to it, not only thought but see by careful attention, diligent watching, the whole movement of thought and the self. You may say all this is too tiresome, perhaps unnecessary. But if you do not pay attention to this, give heed, the future is not only going to be more destructive, more intolerable but without much significance. All this is not a dampening, depressing point of view, it is actually so. What you are now is what you will be in the coming days. You can't avoid it. It is as definite as the sun rising and setting. This is the share of all man, of all humanity, unless we all change, each one of us, change to something that is not projected by thought.

Krishnamurti to Himself

Insight into the Working of the Self

Most human beings are selfish. They are not conscious of their own selfishness; it is the way of their life. And if one is aware that one is selfish, one hides it very carefully and conforms to the pattern of society which is essentially selfish. The selfish mind is very cunning. Either it is brutally and openly selfish or it takes many forms. If you are a politician the selfishness seeks power, status and popularity; it identifies itself with an idea, a mission, and all for the public good. If you are a tyrant it expresses itself in brutal domination. If you are inclined to be religious it takes the form of adoration, devotion, adherence to some belief, some dogma. It also expresses itself in the family; the father pursues his own selfishness in all the ways of his life and so does the mother. Fame, prosperity, good looks form a basis for this hidden, creeping movement of the self. It is in the hierarchical structure of the priesthood, however much they may proclaim their love of God, their adherence to the self-created image of their particular deity. The captains of industry and the poor clerk have this expanding and benumbing sensuality of the self. The monk who has renounced the ways of the world may wander the face of the world or may be locked away in some monastery, but has not left this unending movement of the self. They may change their names, put on robes or take vows of celibacy or silence, but they burn with some ideal, with some image, some symbol.

It is the same with the scientists, with the philosophers, and the professors in the university. The doer of good works, the saints and gurus, the man or the woman who works endlessly for the poor — they all attempt to lose themselves in their work but the work is part of it. They have transferred the egotism to their labours. It begins in childhood and continues to old age. The conceit of knowledge, the practised humility of the leader, the submitting wife and dominating man, all have this disease. The self identifies with the State, with endless groups, with endless ideas and causes, but it remains what it was at the beginning.

Human beings have tried various practices, methods, meditations to be free of this centre which causes so much misery and confusion, but like a shadow it is never captured. It is always there and it slips through your fingers, through your mind. Sometimes it is strengthened or becomes weak according to circumstances. You corner it here, it turns up there.

One wonders if the educator, who is so responsible for a new generation, understands non-verbally what a mischievous thing the self is — how corrupting, distorting, how dangerous it is in our lives. He may not know how to be free of it, he may not even be aware it is there, but once he sees the nature of the movement of the self, can he or she convey its subtleties to the student? And is it not his responsibility to do this? The insight into the working of the self is greater than academic learning. Knowledge can be used by the self for its own expansion, its aggressiveness, its innate cruelty.

Selfishness is the essential problem of our life. Conforming and imitation are part of the self, as is competition and the ruthlessness of talent. If the educator in these schools takes this question to his heart seriously, which I hope he does, then how will he help the student to be selfless? You might say it is a gift of the strange gods or brush it aside as being impossible. But if you are serious, as one must be, and are totally responsible for the student, how will you set about freeing the mind from this ageless, binding energy? — the self which has caused so much sorrow? Would you not, with great care — which implies affection — explain in simple words what the consequences are when he speaks in anger, or when he hits somebody, or when he is thinking of his own importance? Is it not possible to explain to him that when he insists 'this is mine', or boasts 'I did it', or avoids through fear a certain action, he is building a wall, brick by brick, around himself? Is it not possible when his desires, his sensations overpower his rational thinking, to point out that the shadow of the self is growing? Is it not possible to say to him that where the self is, in any guise, there is no love?

But the student might ask the educator, 'Have you realized all this or are you just playing with words?' That very question might awaken your own intelligence and that very intelligence will give you the right feeling and the right words as answer.

As an educator you have no status; you are a human being with all the problems of life like a student. The moment you speak from status, you are actually destroying the human relation. Status implies power and when you are seeking this, consciously or unconsciously, you enter a world of cruelty. You have a great responsibility, my friend, and if you take this total responsibility which is love, then the roots of the self are gone. This is not said as an encouragement or to make you feel that you must do this, but as we are all human beings, representing the whole of mankind, we are totally and wholly responsible whether we choose to be or not. You may try to evade it, but that very movement is the action of the self. Clarity of perception is freedom from the self.

Letters to the Schools

A Benediction of Great Holiness

Early this morning, the sky was without a cloud; the sun was coming up behind the Tuscan hills, grey with olive, with dark cypress. There were no shadows on the river and the aspen leaves were still. A few birds that had not yet migrated were chattering and the river seemed motionless; as the sun came up behind the river it cast long shadows on the quiet water. But a gentle breeze was coming over the hills and through the valleys; it was among the leaves, setting them trembling and dancing with the morning sun on them. There were long and short shadows, fat ones and little ones on the brown, sparkling waters; a solitary chimney began to smoke, grey fumes carrying across the trees. It was a lovely morning, full of enchantment and beauty, there were so many shadows and so many leaves trembling. There was perfume in the air and though it was an autumnal sun there was the breath of spring. A small car was going up the hill, making an awful noise but a thousand shadows remained motionless. It was a lovely morning.

In the afternoon yesterday, it began suddenly, in a room overlooking a noisy street; the strength and the beauty of the otherness was spreading from the room outward over the traffic, past the gardens and beyond the hills. It was there immense and impenetrable; it was there in the afternoon, and just as one was getting into bed it was there with furious intensity, a benediction of great holiness. There is no getting used to it for it is always different, there's something always new, a new quality, a subtle significance, a new light, something that had not been seen before. It was not a thing to be stored up, remembered and examined, at leisure; it was there and no thought could approach for the brain was still and there was no time to experience, to store up. It was there and all thought became still.

The intense energy of life is always there, night and day. It is without friction, without direction, without choice and effort. It is there with such intensity that thought and feeling cannot capture it to mould it according to their fancies, beliefs, experiences and demands. It is there with such abundance that nothing can diminish it. But we try to use it, to give it direction, to capture it within the mould of our existence and thereby twist it to conform to our pattern, experience and knowledge. It is ambition, envy, greed that narrow down its energy and so there is conflict and sorrow; the cruelty of ambition, personal or collective, distorts its intensity, causing hatred, antagonism, conflict. Every action of envy perverts this energy, causing discontent, misery, fear; with fear there is guilt and anxiety and the never-ending misery of comparison and imitation. It is this perverted energy that makes the priest and the general, the politician and the thief. This boundless energy made incomplete by our desire for permanency and security is the soil in which grow barren ideas, competition, cruelty and war; it is the cause of everlasting conflict between man and man.

When all this is put aside, with ease and without effort, then only is there that intense energy which can only exist and flower in freedom. In freedom alone, it causes no conflict and sorrow; then alone it increases and has no end. It is life that has no beginning and no end; it is creation which is love, destruction.

Energy used in one direction leads to one thing, conflict and sorrow; energy that is the expression of total life is bliss beyond measure.

Krishnamurti's Notebook
October 9, 1961

V

Dialogues and Discussions

Is There a God?

Questioner: I really would like to know if there is a God. If there isn't, life has no meaning. Not knowing God, man has invented him in a thousand beliefs and images. The division and the fear bred by all these beliefs have divided him from his fellow-men. To escape the pain and the mischief of this division he creates yet more beliefs, and the mounting misery and confusion have engulfed him. Not knowing, we believe. Can I know God? I've asked this question of many saints both in India and here and they've all emphasized belief. 'Believe and then you will know; without belief you can never know.' What do you think?

KRISHNAMURTI: Is belief necessary to find out? To learn is far more important than to know. Learning about belief is the end of belief. When the mind is free of belief then it can look. It is belief, or disbelief, that binds; for disbelief and belief are the same; they are the opposite sides of the same coin. So we can completely put aside positive or negative belief; the believer and the non-believer are the same. When this actually takes place then the question, 'Is there a God?' has quite a different meaning. The word 'God' with all its tradition, its memory, its intellectual and sentimental connotations — all this is not God. The word is not the real. So can the mind be free of the word?

Questioner: I don't know what that means.

KRISHNAMURTI: The word is the tradition, the hope, the desire to find the absolute, the striving after the ultimate, the movement which gives vitality to existence. So the word itself becomes the ultimate, yet we can see that the word is not the thing. The mind is the word, and the word is thought.

Questioner: And you're asking me to strip myself of the word? How can I do that? The word is the past; it is memory. The wife is the word, and the house is the word. In the beginning was the word. Also the word is the means of communication, identification. Your name is not you, and yet without your name I can't ask about you. And you're asking me if the mind can be free of the word — that is, can the mind be free of its own activity?

KRISHNAMURTI: In the case of the tree the object is before our eyes, and the word refers to the tree by universal agreement. Now, with the word 'God' there is nothing to which it refers, so each man can create his own image of that for which there is no reference. The theologian does it in one way, the intellectual in another, and the believer and the non-believer in their own different ways. Hope generates this belief, and then seeking. This hope is the outcome of despair — the despair of all we see around us in the world. From despair hope is born; they also are two sides of the same coin. When there is no hope there is hell, and this fear of hell gives us the vitality of hope. Then illusion begins. So the word has led us to illusion and not to God at all. God is the illusion which we worship; and the non-believer creates the illusion of another God which he worships — the State, or some utopia, or some book which he thinks contains all truth. So we are asking you whether you can be free of the word with its illusion.

Questioner: I must meditate on this.

KRISHNAMURTI: If there is no illusion, what is left?

Questioner: Only what is.

KRISHNAMURTI: That 'what is' is the most holy.

Questioner: If the 'what is' is the most holy then war is most holy, and hatred, disorder, pain, avarice and plunder. Then we must not speak of any change at all. If 'what is' is sacred, then every murderer and plunderer and exploiter can say, 'Don't touch me, what I'm doing is sacred'.

KRISHNAMURTI: The very simplicity of that statement, '"what is" is the most sacred', leads to great misunderstanding, because we don't see the truth of it. If you see that 'what is' is sacred, you do not murder, you do not make war, you do not hope, you do not exploit. Having done these things you cannot claim immunity from a truth which you have violated. The white man who says to the black rioter, 'what is is sacred, do not interfere, do not burn', has not seen, for if he had, the Negro would be sacred to him, and there would be no need to burn. So if each one of us sees this truth there must be change. The seeing of the truth is change.

Questioner: I came here to find out if there is God, and you have completely confused me.

KRISHNAMURTI: You came to ask if there is God. We said: the word leads to illusion which we worship, and for this illusion we destroy each other willingly. When there is no illusion the 'what is' is most sacred. Now let's look at what actually is. At a given moment the 'what is' may be fear, or utter despair, or a fleeting joy. These things are constantly changing. And also there is the observer who says, 'These things all change around me, but I remain permanent'. Is that a fact, is that what really is? Is he not also changing, adding to and taking away from himself, modifying, adjusting himself, becoming or not becoming? So both the observer and observed are constantly changing. 'What is' is change. That is a fact. That is 'what is'.

Questioner: Then, is love changeable? If everything is a movement of change, isn't love also part of that movement? And if love is changeable, then I can love one woman today and sleep with another tomorrow.

KRISHNAMURTI: Is that love? Or are you saying that love is different from its expression? Or are you giving to expression greater importance than to love, and therefore making a contradiction and a conflict. Can love ever be caught in the wheel of change? If so, then it can also be hate; then love is hate. It is only when there is no illusion that 'what is' is most sacred. When there is no illusion 'what is' is God or any other name that can be used. So God, or whatever name you give it, is when you are not. When you are, it is not. When you are not, love is. When you are, love is not.

The Urgency of Change

Suffering

Questioner: I seem to have suffered a great deal all my life, not physically, but through death and loneliness and the utter futility of my existence. I had a son whom I greatly loved. He died in an accident. My wife left me, and that caused a great deal of pain. I suppose I am like thousands of other middle-class people with sufficient money and a steady job. I'm not complaining of my circumstances but I want to understand what sorrow means, why it comes at all. One has been told that wisdom comes through sorrow, but I have found quite the contrary.

KRISHNAMURTI: I wonder what you have learnt from suffering? Have you learnt anything at all? What has sorrow taught you?

Questioner: It has certainly taught me never to be attached to people, and a certain bitterness, a certain aloofness, and not to allow my feelings to run away with me. It has taught me to be very careful not to get hurt again.

KRISHNAMURTI: So, as you say, it hasn't taught you wisdom; on the contrary it has made you more cunning, more insensitive. Does sorrow teach one anything at all except the obvious self-protective reactions?

Questioner: I have always accepted suffering as part of my life, but I feel now, somehow, that I'd like to be free of it, free of all the tawdry bitterness and indifference without again going through all the pain of attachment. My life is so pointless and empty, utterly self-enclosed and insignificant. It's a life of mediocrity, and perhaps that mediocrity is the greatest sorrow of all.

KRISHNAMURTI: There is the personal sorrow and the sorrow of the world. There is the sorrow of ignorance and the sorrow of time. This ignorance is the lack of knowing oneself, and the sorrow of time is the deception that time can cure, heal and change. Most people are caught in that deception and either worship sorrow or explain it away. But in either case it continues, and one never asks oneself if it can come to an end.

Questioner: But I am asking now if it can come to an end, and how? How am I to end it? I understand that it's no good running away from it, or resisting it with bitterness and cynicism. What am I to do to end the grief which I have carried for so long?

KRISHNAMURTI: Self-pity is one of the elements of sorrow. Another element is being attached to someone and encouraging or fostering his attachment to you. Sorrow is not only there when attachment fails you but its seed is in the very beginning of that attachment. In all this the trouble is the utter lack of knowing oneself. Knowing oneself is the ending of sorrow. We are afraid to know ourselves because we have divided ourselves into the good and the bad, the evil and the noble, the pure and the impure. The good is always judging the bad, and these fragments are at war with each other. This war is sorrow. To end sorrow is to see the fact and not invent its opposite, for the opposites contain each other. Walking in this corridor of opposites is sorrow. This fragmentation of life into the high and the low, the noble and the ignoble, God and the Devil, breeds conflict and pain. When there is sorrow, there is no love. Love and sorrow cannot live together.

Questioner: Ah! But love can inflict sorrow on another. I may love another and yet bring him sorrow.

KRISHNAMURTI: Do you bring it, if you love, or does he? If another is attached to you, with or without encouragement, and you turn away from him and he suffers, is it you or he who has brought about his suffering?

Questioner: You mean I am not responsible for someone else's sorrow, even if it is on my account? How does sorrow ever end then?

KRISHNAMURTI: As we have said, it is only in knowing oneself completely that sorrow ends. Do you know yourself at a glance, or hope to after a long analysis? Through analysis you cannot know yourself. You can only know yourself without accumulation, in relationship, from moment to moment. This means that one must be aware, without any choice, of what is actually taking place. It means to see oneself as one is, without the opposite, the ideal, without the knowledge of what one has been. If you look at yourself with the eyes of resentment or rancour then what you see is coloured by the past. The shedding of the past all the time when you see yourself is the freedom from the past. Sorrow ends only when there is the light of understanding, and this light is not lit by one experience or by one flash of understanding: this understanding is lighting itself all the time. Nobody can give it to you — no book, trick, teacher or saviour. The understanding of yourself is the ending of sorrow.

The Urgency of Change

The Religious Life

Questioner: I should like to know what a religious life is. I have stayed in monasteries for several months, meditated, led a disciplined life, read a great deal. I've been to various temples, churches and mosques. I've tried to lead a very simple, harmless life, trying not to hurt people or animals. This surely isn't all there is to a religious life? I've practised yoga, studied Zen and followed many religious disciplines. I am, and have always been, a vegetarian. As you see, I'm getting old now, and I've lived with some of the saints in different parts of the world, but somehow I feel that all this is only the outskirts of the real thing. So I wonder if we can discuss today what to you is a religious life.

KRISHNAMURTI: A sannyasi came to see me one day and he was sad. He said he had taken a vow of celibacy and left the world to become a mendicant, wandering from village to village, but his sexual desires were so imperious that one morning he decided to have his sexual organs surgically removed. For many months he was in constant pain, but somehow it healed, and after many years he fully realized what he had done. And so he came to see me and in that little room he asked me what he could do now, having mutilated himself, to become normal again — not physically, of course, but inwardly. He had done this thing because sexual activity was considered contrary to a religious life. It was considered mundane, belonging to the world of pleasure which a real sannyasi must at all costs avoid. He said: 'Here I am, feeling completely lost, deprived of my manhood. I struggled so hard against my sexual desires, trying to control them, and ultimately this terrible thing took place. Now what am I to do? I know that what I did was wrong. My energy has almost gone and I seem to be ending my life in darkness.' He held my hand, and we sat silently for some time.

Is this a religious life? Is the denial of pleasure or beauty a way that leads to a religious life? To deny the beauty of the skies and the hills and the human form, will that lead to a religious life? But that is what most saints and monks believe. They torture themselves in that belief. Can a tortured, twisted, distorted mind ever find what is a religious life? Yet all religions assert that the only way to reality or to God, or whatever they call it, is through this torture, this distortion. They all make the distinction between what they call a spiritual or religious life and what they call a worldly life.

A man who lives only for pleasure, with occasional flashes of sorrow and piety, whose whole life is given to amusement and entertainment is, of course, a worldly man, although he may also be very clever, very scholarly, and fill his life with other people's thoughts or his own. And a man who has a gift and exercises it for the benefit of society, or for his own pleasure, and who achieves fame in the fulfilment of that gift, such a man, surely, is also worldly. But it is also worldly to go to church, or to the temple or the mosque, to pray, steeped in prejudice, bigotry, utterly unaware of the brutality that this implies. It is worldly to be patriotic, nationalistic, idealistic. The man who shuts himself up in a monastery — getting up at regular hours with a book in hand, reading and praying — is surely also worldly. And the man who goes out to do good works, whether he is a social reformer or a missionary, is just like the politician in his concern with the world. The division between the religious life and the world is the very essence of worldliness. The minds of all these people — monks, saints, reformers — are not very different from the minds of those who are only concerned with the things that give pleasure.

So it is important not to divide life into the worldly and the non-worldly. It is important not to make the distinction between the worldly and the so-called religious. Without the world of matter, the material world, we wouldn't be here. Without the beauty of the sky and the single tree on the hill, without that woman going by and that man riding the horse, life wouldn't be possible. We are concerned with the totality of life and not a particular part of it which is considered religious in opposition to the rest. So one begins to see that a religious life is concerned with the whole and not with the particular.

Questioner: I understand what you say. We have to deal with the totality of living; we can't separate the world from the so-called spirit. So the question is: in what way can we act religiously with regard to all the things in life?

KRISHNAMURTI: What do we mean by acting religiously? Don't you mean a way of life in which there is no division — division between the worldly and the religious, between what should be and what shouldn't be, between me and you, between like and dislike? This division is conflict. A life of conflict is not a religious life. A religious life is only possible when we deeply understand conflict. This understanding is intelligence. It is this intelligence that acts rightly. What most people call intelligence is merely deftness in some technical activity, or cunning in business or political chicanery.

Questioner: So my question really means how is one to live without conflict, and bring about that feeling of true sanctity which is not simply emotional piety conditioned by some religious cage — no matter how old and venerated that cage is?

KRISHNAMURTI: A man living without too much conflict in a village, or dreaming in a cave on a 'sacred' hillside, is surely not living the religious life that we are talking about. To end conflict is one of the most complex things. It needs self-observation and the sensitivity of awareness of the outer as well as of the inner. Conflict can only end where there is the understanding of the contradiction in oneself. This contradiction will always exist if there is no freedom from the known, which is the past. Freedom from the past means living in the now which is not of time, in which there is only this movement of freedom, untouched by the past, by the known.

Questioner: What do you mean by freedom from the past?

KRISHNAMURTI: The past is all our accumulated memories. These memories act in the present and create our hopes and fears of the future. These hopes and fears are the psychological future; without them there is no future. So the present is the action of the past, and the mind is this movement of the past. The past acting in the present creates what we call the future. This response of the past is involuntary, it is not summoned or invited, it is upon us before we know it.

Questioner: In that case, how are we going to be free of it?

KRISHNAMURTI: To be aware of this movement without choice — because choice again is more of this same movement of the past — is to observe the past in action: such observation is not a movement of the past. To observe without the image of thought is action in which the past has ended. To observe the tree without thought is action without the past. To observe the action of the past is again action without the past. The state of seeing is more important than what is seen. To be aware of the past in that choiceless observation is not only to act differently, but to be different. In this awareness memory acts without impediment, and efficiently. To be religious is to be so choicelessly aware that there is freedom from the known even whilst the known acts wherever it has to.

Questioner: But the known, the past, still sometimes acts even when it should not; it still acts to cause conflict.

KRISHNAMURTI: To be aware of this is also to be in a state of inaction with regard to the past which is acting. So freedom from the known is truly the religious life. That doesn't mean to wipe out the known but to enter a different dimension altogether from which the known is observed. This action of seeing choicelessly is the action of love. The religious life is this action, and all living is this action, and the religious mind is this action. So religion, and the mind, and life, and love, are one.

The Urgency of Change

On the True Denial

Teacher: In one of your talks to the children you said that when a problem arises, one should solve it immediately. How is one to do this?

KRISHNAMURTI: To solve a problem immediately, you have to understand the problem. Is the understanding of a problem a matter of time or is it a matter of intensity of perception, an intensity of seeing? Let us say that I have a problem: I am vain. It is a problem with me in the sense that it creates a conflict, a contradiction within me. It is a fact that I am vain and there is also another fact that I do not want to be vain. Firstly, I have to understand the fact that I am vain. I have to live with that fact. I must not only be intensely aware of the fact but comprehend it fully. Now, is comprehension a matter of time? I can see the fact immediately, can't I? And the immediacy of perception, of seeing, dissolves the fact. When I see a cobra there is immediate action. But I do not see vanity in the same way — when I see vanity either I like it and therefore I continue with it, or I do not want it because it creates conflict. If it does not create conflict there is no problem.

Perception and understanding are not of time. Perception is a matter of intensity of seeing, a seeing that is total. What is the nature of seeing something totally? What gives one the capacity, the energy, the vitality, the drive, to deal with something immediately, with all one's undivided energy? The moment you have divided energy you have conflict and therefore there is no seeing, there is no perception of something total. Now, what gives you the energy to make you jump when you see a cobra? What are the processes that make the organic as well as the psychological, the whole being jump, so that there is no hesitation, so that the reaction is immediate? What has gone into that immediacy? Several things have gone into that action which is immediate: fear, natural protection, which must be there, the knowledge that the cobra is a deadly thing.

Now, why have we not the same energetic action with regard to the dissolution of vanity? I am taking vanity as an example. There are several reasons that have gone into my lack of energy. I like vanity; the world is based on it; it is the basis of the social pattern; it gives me a certain sense of vitality, a certain quality of dignity and aloofness, a sense that I am a little better than another. All this prevents that energy which is necessary to dissolve vanity. Now, either I analyse all the reasons which have prevented my action, prevented my having energy to deal with vanity, or I see immediately. Analysis is a process of time and a process of postponement. While I am analysing, vanity continues and time is not going to end it. So I have to see vanity totally and I lack the energy to see. Now, to gather the dissipated energy requires a gathering not only when I am confronted with a problem such as vanity, but a gathering all the time, even when there is no problem. We do not have problems all the time. There are moments when we have no problems. If at those moments we are gathering energy, gathering in the sense of being aware, then when the problem arises, we can meet it and not go through the process of analysis.

Teacher: There is another difficulty: when there is no problem, and no gathering of this energy, some form of mentation is going on.

KRISHNAMURTI: There is a waste of energy in mere repetition, reaction to memory, reaction to experience. If you observe your own mind you will see that a pleasurable incident keeps on repeating itself. You want to go back to it, you want to think about it, and so it gathers momentum.

When the mind is aware there is no wastage, is it possible to let that momentum, to let that thought flower? Which means never to say, 'This is right or wrong', but to live the thought over, to have a feeling in which the thought can flourish so that by itself it will come to an end.

Should we approach the problem differently? We have been talking about creating a generation with a new quality of mind. How do we do this? If I were a teacher here, it would be my concern — and a good educator obviously has this concern at heart — to bring about a new mind, a new sensitivity, a new feeling for the trees, the skies, the heavens, the streams; to bring into being a new consciousness, not the old consciousness remoulded into a new shape. I mean a totally new mind, uncontaminated by the past. If that is my concern, how do I set about it?

First of all, is it possible to bring about such a new mind? Not a mind which is a continuity of the past in a new mould but a mind that is uncontaminated. Is it feasible, or must the past continue through the present to be modified and be put into a new mould? In which case there is no new generation; it is the older generation repeated in a new form.

I think it is possible to create a new generation. And I ask: How am I not only to experience this within myself, but to express it to the student?

If I see something experimentally in myself I cannot miss expressing it to the student. Surely, it is not a question of I and the other, but a mutual thing, isn't it?

Now, how do I bring about a mind that is uncontaminated? You and I are not newborn; we have been contaminated by society, by Hinduism, by education, by the family, by society, by newspapers. How do we break through the contamination? Do I say it is part of my existence and accept it? What do I do, sir? Here is a problem — that our minds are contaminated. For the older ones it is more difficult to break through. You are comparatively young and the problem is to uncontaminate the mind; how is it to be done?

Either it is possible or it is not possible. Now, how is one to discover whether it is or not? I would like you to jump into it.

Do you know what is meant by the word 'denial'? What does it mean to deny the past, to deny being a Hindu? What do you mean by that word 'deny'? Have you ever denied anything? There is a true denial and a false denial. The denial with a motive is a false denial. The denial with a purpose, the denial with an intention, with an eye on the future, is not a denial. If I deny something in order to get something more, it is not denial. But there is a denial which has no motive. When I deny and do not know what is in store for me in the future, that is true denial. I deny being a Hindu, I deny belonging to any organization, I deny any particular creed and in that very denial I make myself completely insecure. Do you know such a denial, and have you ever denied anything? Can you deny the past that way — deny, not knowing what is in the future? Can you deny the known?

Teacher: When I deny something, say Hinduism, there is a simultaneous understanding of what Hinduism is.

KRISHNAMURTI: What we were discussing is the bringing about of a new mind and if it is possible. A mind that is contaminated cannot be a new mind. So we are talking of de-contamination, and whether that is possible. And in relation to that I began by asking what you mean by denial, because I think denial has a great deal to do with it. Denial has to do with a new mind. If I deny cleanly, without roots, without motive, it is real denial. Now, is that possible? You see, if I do not completely deny society in which is involved politics, economics, social relationships, ambition, greed — if I do not deny all that completely, it is impossible to find out what it is to have a new mind. Therefore the first breaking of the foundation is the denial of the things I have known. Is that possible?

Obviously, drugs will not bring about a new mind; nothing will bring it about except a total denial of the past. Is it possible? What do you say? And if I have felt the perfume, the sight, the taste of such denial, how do I help to convey it to a student? He must have in abundance the known — mathematics, geography, history — and yet be abundantly free of the known, remorselessly free of it.

Teacher: Sir, all sensations leave a residue, a disturbance which lead to various kinds of conflict and other forms of mental activity. The traditional approach of all religions is to deny this sensation by discipline and denial. But in what you say there seems to be a heightened receptivity to these sensations so that you see the sensations without distortion or residue.

KRISHNAMURTI: That is the issue. Sensitivity and sensation are two different things. A mind that is a slave to thought, sensation, feeling, is a residual mind. It enjoys the residue, it enjoys thinking about the pleasurable world, and each thought leaves a mark, which is the residue. Each thought of a certain pleasure you have had leaves a mark which makes for insensitivity. It obviously dulls the mind, and discipline, control and suppression further dull the mind. I am saying that sensitivity is not sensation, that sensitivity implies no mark, no residue. So what is the question?

Teacher: Is the denial of which you are speaking different from a denial which is the restriction of sensation?

KRISHNAMURTI: How do you see those flowers, see the beauty of them, be completely sensitive to them so that there is no residue, no memory of them, so that when you see them again an hour later you see a new flower? That is not possible if you see as a sensation and that sensation is associated with flowers, with pleasure. The traditional way is to shut out what is pleasurable because such associations awaken other forms of pleasure and so you discipline yourself not to look. To cut association with a surgical knife is immature. So how is the mind, how are the eyes, to see the tremendous colour and yet have it leave no mark?

I am not asking for a method. How does that state come into being? Otherwise we cannot be sensitive. It is like a photographic plate which receives impressions and is self-renewing. It is exposed, and yet becomes negative for the next impression. So all the time, it is self-cleansing of every pleasure. Is that possible or are we playing with words and not with facts?

The fact which I see clearly is that any residual sensitivity, sensation, dulls the mind. I deny that fact, but I do not know what it is to be so extraordinarily sensitive that experience leaves no mark and yet to see the flower with fullness, with tremendous intensity. I see as an undeniable fact that every sensation, every feeling, every thought, leaves a mark, shapes the mind, and that such marks cannot possibly bring about a new mind. I see that to have a mind with marks is death, so I deny death. But I do not know the other. I also see that a good mind is sensitive without the residue of experience. It experiences, but the experience leaves no mark from which it draws further experiences, further conclusions, further death.

The one I deny and the other I do not know. How is this transition from the denial of the known to the unknown to come into being?

How does one deny? Does one deny the known, not in great dramatic incidents but in little incidents? Do I deny when I am shaving and I remember the lovely time I had in

Switzerland? Does one deny the remembrance of a pleasant time? Does one grow aware of it and deny it? That is not dramatic, it is not spectacular, nobody knows about it. Still this constant denial of little things, the little wipings, the little rubbings off, not just one great, big wiping away is essential. It is essential to deny thought as remembrance, pleasant or unpleasant, every minute of the day as it arises. One is doing it not for any motive, not in order to enter into the extraordinary state of the unknown. You live in Rishi Valley and think of Bombay or Rome. This creates a conflict, makes the mind dull, a divided thing. Can you see this and wipe it away? Can you keep on wiping away not because you want to enter into the unknown? You can never know what the unknown is because the moment you recognize it as the unknown you are back in the known.

The process of recognition is a process of the continued known. As I do not know what the unknown is, I can only do this one thing, keep on wiping thought away as it arises.

You see that flower, feel it, see the beauty, the intensity, the extraordinary brilliance of it. Then you go to the room in which you live, which is not well proportioned, which is ugly. You live in the room but you have a certain sense of beauty and you begin to think of the flower, and you pick up the thought as it arises and you wipe it away. Now, from what depth do you wipe, from what depth do you deny the flower, your wife, your gods, your economic life? You have to live with your wife, your children, with this ugly monstrous society. You cannot withdraw from life. But when you deny totally thought, sorrow, pleasure, your relationship is different and so there must a total denial, not a partial denial, not a keeping of the things which you like and a denying of the things which you do not like.

Now, how do you translate what you have understood to the student?

Teacher: You have said that in teaching and learning, the situation is one of intensity where you do not say, 'I am teaching you something'. Now, this constant wiping away of the marks of thought — has it something to do with the intensity of the teaching-learning situation?

KRISHNAMURTI: Obviously. You see, I feel that teaching and learning are both the same. What is taking place here? I am not teaching you — I am not your teacher or authority, I am merely exploring and conveying my exploration to you. You can take it or leave it. The position is the same with regard to students.

Teacher: What is the teacher then to do?

KRISHNAMURTI: You can only find out when you are constantly denying. Have you ever tried it? It is as if you cannot sleep for a single minute during the day time.

Teacher: It not only needs energy, sir, but also releases a lot of energy.

KRISHNAMURTI: But first you must have the energy to deny.

Krishnamurti on Education

Enlightenment

Questioner: All so-called religious people have something in common and I see this same thing in most of the people who come to hear you. They are all looking for something which they variously call nirvana, liberation, enlightenment, self-realization, eternity or God. Their goal is defined and held before them in various teachings, and each of these teachings, these systems, has its set of sacred books, its disciplines, its teachers, its morality, its philosophy, its promises and threats — a straight and narrow path excluding the rest of the world and promising at its end some heaven or other. Most of these seekers move from one system to another, substituting the latest teaching for the one they have recently dropped. They move from one emotional orgy to another, not thinking that the same process is at work in all this seeking. Some of them remain in one system with one group and refuse to budge. Others eventually believe that they have realized whatever it is they wanted to realize, and then they spend their days in some withdrawn beatitude attracting in their turn a group of disciples who start the whole cycle over again. In all this there is the compulsive greed to attain some realization and, usually, the bitter disappointment and frustration of failure. All this seems to me very unhealthy. These people sacrifice ordinary living for some imaginary goal and a most unpleasant feeling emanates from this kind of milieu: fanaticism, hysteria, violence and stupidity. One is surprised to find among them certain good writers who otherwise seem quite sane. All this is called religion. The whole thing stinks to high heaven. This is the incense of piety. I have observed it everywhere. This search for enlightenment causes great havoc and people are sacrificed in its wake. Now, I would like to ask you, is there in fact any such thing as enlightenment, and if so, what is it?

KRISHNAMURTI: If it is an escape from everyday living, everyday living being the extraordinary movement of relationship, then this so-called realization, this so-called enlightenment, or whatever name you like to give it, is illusion and hypocrisy. Anything that denies love and the understanding of life and action is bound to create a great deal of mischief, it distorts the mind, and life is made a horrible affair. So if we take that to be axiomatic then perhaps we may proceed to find out if enlightenment — whatever that may mean — can be found in the very act of living. After all, living is more important than any idea, ideal, goal or principle. It is because we don't know what living is that we invent these visionary, unrealistic concepts which offer escape. The real question is, can one find enlightenment in living, in the everyday activities of life, or is it only for the few who are endowed with some extraordinary capacity to discover this beatitude? Enlightenment means to be a light unto oneself, but a light which is not self-projected or imagined, which is not some personal idiosyncrasy. After all, this has always been the teaching of true religion, though not of organized belief and fear.

Questioner: You say the teaching of true religion! This immediately creates the camp of the professionals and specialists versus the rest of the world. Do you mean, then, that religion is separate from life?

KRISHNAMURTI: Religion is not separate from life; on the contrary it is life itself. It is this division between religion and life which has bred all the misery you are talking about. So we come back to the basic question of whether it is possible in daily life to live in a state which, for the moment, let us call enlightenment?

Questioner: I still don't know what you mean by enlightenment.

KRISHNAMURTI: A state of negation. Negation is the most positive action, not positive assertion. This is a very important thing to understand. Most of us so easily accept positive dogma, a positive creed, because we want to be secure, to belong, to be attached, to depend. The positive attitude divides and brings about duality. The conflict then begins between this attitude and others. But the negation of all values, of all morality, of all beliefs, having no frontiers, cannot be in opposition to anything. A positive statement in its very definition separates, and separation is resistance. To this we are accustomed, this is our conditioning. To deny all this is not immoral; on the contrary to deny all division and resistance is the highest morality. To negate everything that man has invented, to negate all his values, ethics and gods, is to be in a state of mind in which there is no duality, therefore no resistance or conflict between opposites. In this state there are no opposites, and this state is not the opposite of something else.

Questioner: Then how do you know what is good and what is bad? Or is there no good and bad? What is to prevent me from crime or even murder? If I have no standards, what is to prevent me from God knows what aberrations?

KRISHNAMURTI: To deny all this is to deny oneself, and oneself is the conditioned entity who continually pursues a conditioned good. To most of us negation appears as a vacuum because we know activity only in the prison of our conditioning, fear and misery. From that we look at negation and imagine it to be some terrible state of oblivion or emptiness. To the man who has negated all the assertions of society, religion, culture and morality, the man who is still in the prison of social conformity is a man of sorrow. Negation is the state of enlightenment which functions in all the activities of a man who is free of the past. It is the past, with its tradition and its authority, that has to be negated. Negation is freedom, and it is the free man who lives, loves, and knows what it means to die.

Questioner: That much is clear; but you say nothing about any intimation of the transcendental, the divine, or whatever you like to call it.

KRISHNAMURTI: The intimation of that can be found only in freedom, and any statement about it is the denial of freedom; any statement about it becomes a verbal communication without meaning. It is there, but it cannot be found or invited, least of all imprisoned in any system, or ambushed by any clever tricks of the mind. It is not in the churches or the temples or the mosques. There is no path to it, no guru, no system that can reveal its beauty; its ecstasy comes only when there is love. This is enlightenment.

Questioner: Does it bring any new understanding of the nature of the universe or of consciousness or being? All the religious texts are full of that sort of thing.

KRISHNAMURTI: It is like asking questions about the other shore while living and suffering on this shore. When you are on the other shore you are everything and nothing, and you never ask such questions. All such questions are of this shore and really have no meaning at all. Begin to live and you will be there without asking, without seeking, without fear.

Conversations

Sources and Acknowledgements

Four Public Talks in Bombay 1967, from *The Collected Works of J. Krishnamurti*, vol. XVII. © 1991 Krishnamurti Foundation of America.

Questions and Answers from New Delhi Talk, 14 November 1948; New Delhi Talk, 19 December 1948; London Talk, 23 October 1949; from *The Collected Works of J. Krishnamurti,* vol. V. © 1991 Krishnamurti Foundation of America.

Questions and Answers from Colombo Talk, 1 January 1950; Colombo Talk, 8 January 1950; London Talk, 15 April 1952; from *The Collected Works of J. Krishnamurti*, vol. VI. © 1991 Krishnamurti Foundation of America.

Questions and Answers from Bombay Talk, 15 February 1953; Ojai Talk, 10 August 1952; from *The Collected Works of J. Krishnamurti,* vol. VII. © 1991 Krishnamurti Foundation of America.

Questions and Answers from Bombay Talk, 10 February 1954; Bombay Talk, 20 February 1955; from *The Collected Works of J. Krishnamurti,* vol. VIII. © 1991 Krishnamurti Foundation of America.

Questions and Answers from Amsterdam Talk, 19 May 1955; Amsterdam Talk, 26 May 1955; Ojai Talk, 14 August 1955; Ojai Talk, 21 August 1955; Bombay Talk, 25 March 1956; Bombay Talk, 28 March 1956; from *The Collected Works of J. Krishnamurti*, vol. IX. © 1991 Krishnamurti Foundation of America.

Questions and Answers from Hamburg Talk, 15 September 1956; New Delhi Talk, 10 October 1956; from *The Collected Works of J. Krishnamurti,* vol. X. © 1991 Krishnamurti Foundation of America.

Question and Answer from Saanen Talk, 19 July 1966, from *The Collected Works of J. Krishnamurti,* vol. XVI. © 1991 Krishnamurti Foundation of America.

‘Problems and Escapes’, ‘Obsession’, ‘Security’, ‘Anger’ and ‘Self-esteem’, from *Commentaries on Living.* © 1956 Krishnamurti Foundation of America.

‘Conditioning’ and ‘The Storm in the Mind’, from *Commentaries on Living, Second Series,* © 1958 Krishnamurti Foundation of America.

‘Enlightenment’ (Chapter 7), from *Conversations.* © 1970 Krishnamurti Foundation Trust, Ltd.

‘Why is There this Sorrow of Death? (Chapter 4), from *The Only Revolution.* © 1970 Krishnamurti Foundation Trust, Ltd.

‘Is there a God?’, ‘Suffering’, ‘The Religious Life’, from *The Urgency of Change.* © 1970 Krishnamurti Foundation Trust. Ltd.

‘On the True Denial’, from *Krishnamurti on Education.* © 1974 Krishnamurti Foundation Trust, Ltd.

‘A Benediction of Great Holiness’ (Pages 136-137), from *Krishnamurti's Notebook.* © 1976 Krishnamurti Foundation Trust, Ltd.

‘A Feeling for All Living Things’ (Pages 9-10), ‘What is the Future of Mankind?’ (Pages 45-49), from *Krishnamurti to Himself.* © 1987 Krishnamurti Foundation Trust, Ltd.

‘Insight into the Working of the Self (Pages 59-61), from *Letters to the Schools.* © 1981 Krishnamurti Foundation Trust, Ltd.

Question and Answer, from *Meeting Life.* © 1993 Krishnamurti Foundation Trust, Ltd.